the

rebel

cook

To Deb,
Very best wishes,
Linda

Linda Kupecek

the

rebel

cook

entertaining advice for the clueless

ALTITUDE PUBLISHING

Published by Altitude Publishing Canada Ltd.
1500 Railway Avenue, Canmore, Alberta T1W 1P6
www.altitudepublishing.com
www.amazingstories.ca
1-800-957-6888

PUBLISHER: Stephen Hutchings
ASSOCIATE PUBLISHER: Kara Turner
EDITOR: Lori Burwash
DESIGNER: Bryan Pezzi

We acknowledge the financial support of the Government of
Canada through the Book Publishing Industry Development
Program (BPIDP) for our publishing activities.

ALTITUDE GREENTREE PROGRAM
Altitude Publishing will plant twice as many trees
as were used in the manufacturing of this product.

LIBRARY AND ARCHIVES CANADA CATALOGUING IN PUBLICATION DATA

Kupecek, Linda
    Rebel cook / Linda Kupecek.

ISBN 1-55153-938-1

    1. Entertaining--Humor. I. Title.

TX731.K85 2006   642.4'0207   C2006-904970-X

Printed and bound in Canada by Friesens
2 4 6 8 9 7 5 3 1

To my mother, Julia, who, unlike me, is a wonderful cook and makes magic in the kitchen

contents

introduction

I love to entertain. My heart is warmed like a perfectly coddled egg by the sights and sounds of my friends around my dining room table, laughing, talking, eating, and drinking. Yes, I love to invite people to dinner.

Unfortunately, once you invite them to dinner, they make certain unfortunate assumptions.

For example, that you will serve them food.

The more experienced and battle-scarred of my friends might be relieved if I invited them to dinner and forgot the food. For, alas, I am an imperfect cook. Perhaps I should state that a little more strongly. I am a Rebel Cook. I am incapable of serving a meal that looks like anything that Martha Stewart, or any other of the

9

annoying celebrity chefs and homemakers so prevalent in the media, would serve. These people, with their ultra-perfect competence, have made life in the kitchen impossible for those of us with two left spoons. No wonder some of them landed up in jail. I meant to send a leaden fruitcake to the prison.

I am shaken and stunned by all that culinary brilliance. I wander, bewildered and beleaguered, through the kitchen, gamely struggling with recipes that never (ever) turn out as they should. However, it must be said: I have recognized my incompetence and am defiantly unapologetic. Hence, my stance as the Rebel Cook.

The kitchen is a battlefield for people like me. On the one side, there are traditions. There are expectations. There are the appliances and the chickens and the vegetables that lie about on the counter mocking me. There are tremendous pressures on me, the hostess, to deliver a meal. On the other side of the battlefield of weathered linoleum and tomato-spattered walls is ME — alone — the Rebel Cook. My only ally? My sense of humour.

Do not think, dear reader, that I am defeated. That I will hang my head in shame just because I have brought people to tears with my culinary defeats. In one case, my mother, who after taking a bite of what was supposed to be a cake, turned to me after an interminable three minutes of chewing and said, feelingly, with tears in her eyes, "Darling, with all your brains and talent, don't waste your precious energy in the kitchen."

Then there was the gentleman friend who, on viewing what I now recognize as a crime against an innocent bundle of asparagus, sat mutely at the table, his downcast eyes filled with salty liquid commentary.

I have stunned, terrified, and stopped clocks with what I have presented at table, yet I still entertain. I call. And they come. Like lemmings.

Amazingly, I am told that people love to come to my place. And maybe not to laugh at my cooking. With that in mind, I presume to share the secrets of my rumoured success as an eccentric hostess.

I know there are others out there like me, desperately trying to deliver meals when all odds are against them. And there must be even more who never entertain because of the fear of failure. One of the joys of life, in my opinion, is to share your home and your hospitality, to fete people, make them feel welcome and valued. In my youth, I was terrified of entertaining. I was smart enough to know I was a lousy cook, beyond

redemption. Any recipe, in my hands, turned to disaster. Or worse. Pablum. Dry crusted fossil. Mush. Bitter gruel. I have had consistent and infallible moments of brilliance when I have mutated expensive cuts of meat, exquisite vegetables, and gold-plated ingredients into the inedible. It is a constant in the universe. I am a lousy cook.

In my defence, I may be meditating over the stove. Or perhaps dreaming up dialogue for a screenplay. I may have been building a relationship with the pumpkin and am reluctant to attack it with knife or spices. Or perhaps I am in the throes of a panic attack. Sometimes I start to read a recipe, then the walls start to jiggle, everything goes black, and when I come to, I have eaten an entire box of chocolate truffles and drunk whatever is in the fridge (if I am lucky, chardonnay, if not, a litre of vanilla soy milk). The kitchen may burn down around me, but I am otherwise occupied.

Nevertheless, it occurred to me that if I wanted to be invited out into society, I had better start entertaining. And if I didn't kill off a large contingent of my friends, perhaps I might have a social life.

This, then, is the premise of this book. It is a call to arms, an invocation of the kitchen gods, and a cry to rebellion for all of you out there who, like me, were once afraid to entertain. You may have a nervous collapse doing it, but you can serve dinner to friends and emerge relatively unscathed. So will they, if you don't accidentally cook the rice in vinegar instead of water.

If you are a foodie (I love foodies and am flattered that some people actually think I am a foodie just because I write for a food magazine), then I must emit some warnings.

My experience with foodies is that they will forgive much if the food is good. I am not this sort of person. I have been hauled into restaurants that seemed as if they would be a good choice for a death scene in *The Godfather* and into dingy cafes that could be on the regular route of the health authorities, and I have not been amused. I am not willing to risk my life for the perfect pesto.

If you are the sort of person who loves good food so much that you are willing to go to restaurants with cracked linoleum on the floor and rats biting your ankles and dine on food that may or may not be a family pet, but you don't care, because it tastes so good, then stop reading right now. Your standards are too high for this book. You are a foodie, and you love food, and you can probably cook, too. You don't need to read this book. Just go on your merry way and enjoy your life.

This book is intended for the desperate, the demented, and the innocent: those who, like me, don't have a clue.

I have made just about every mistake to be made

in the kitchen and in the dining room. I have humiliated myself umpteen times with the horrors I have presented at table. I have wept desperately over curmudgeonly chickens and limp salads. I have stood, frozen with shock, as microwaves exploded, chickens imploded, and pots erupted all around me.

But I am a Rebel Cook. I have learned, deviously, carefully, cleverly, how to invite people to my place and show them a good time, without any skills whatsoever in the kitchen. And I am about to share them with you.

However, because I am giving away all my secrets, I hope that you will buy at least 10 copies of this book and send them to friends (in other cities) in exchange for the fact that my reputation will be ruined. Now everybody will know how I have managed to walk the tightrope of culinary incompetence and successful entertaining. (Note: my definition of "successful entertaining" is a night where nobody passes out after the first sip of soup, and nobody — especially me — gets sued.)

Please forgive any overstatements or generalizations. Bear in mind that I am a desperate woman, trying to be a Gracious Hostess at any cost, as long as I

rules to ensure a perfect meal

- That the number of guests does not exceed a dozen, so that conversation can constantly be general.
- That they should be carefully chosen, that their professions be different but their tastes similar and with such points of contact that one will not have to resort to the odious formality of presentations.
- That the dining room be luxuriously lit, the cloth be of the utmost cleanliness, and the temperature from thirteen to sixteen degrees by the Reaumur thermometer (sixty one to sixty six degrees F.)
- That the men be witty without pretensions and the women charming without being too coquettish.
- That the choice of dishes should be exquisite but restrained in number and the wines be of the first quality, each the best of its kind.
- That the order, for the former, should be from the most substantial to the lightest and, for the latter, from the lightest to those with the greatest bouquet.
- That the speed of eating should be moderate, dinner being the last affair of the day, and that the guests behave like travelers who aim to arrive at the same destination together.

Jean-Anthelme Brillat-Savarin, *La Physiologie du goût* (1826) don't have to be a good cook. I have bungled my way through countless dinner parties and behaved just as badly as any boor unveiled in this book. I am sharing my sins in a generous and noble effort to improve the world. Also note that I take no responsibility for the few recipes included in the book. The fact that I haven't killed anybody so far is just a wild bit of luck.

I celebrate the Rebel Cook — the man or woman who rebels against the notion that only fabulous cooks should entertain. We Rebel Cooks have the right to run amok in the kitchen and then emerge, proudly bearing a platter of the Unknown Creation, with our heads held high.

Take heart. If somebody as klutzy and nutsy in the kitchen as I am can entertain and not be drummed out of town — anybody can. Read on ...

guess who's coming to dinner?

"To invite someone is to take charge of his happiness during the time he spends under your roof."

JEAN-ANTHELME BRILLAT-SAVARIN,
LA PHYSIOLOGIE DU GOÛT (1826)

To me, the key component of any dinner party is not the food. In my home, the most important ingredients are the people. Why does one entertain? We invite people to our homes because we want to give them the gift of our attention and generosity.

Some of my most joyous moments have been at the home of my friend the collector, who, with the greatest of care, serves course after course of exquisitely prepared food, bringing out his best sterling and china to make the event an occasion. What makes it meaningful is the humanity, the loving care with which he makes me feel a valued and honoured guest.

If all one wants to do is present a perfect meal and then sit in silence with the coq au vin, why not plant a pile of plush animals around the table and enjoy? If one wants conversation, and is not a multiple personality, it follows that one must consider inviting people. Real, live people who speak multi-syllabically.

But a word of advice: Don't invite just anybody. One is creating a social event, not a hodgepodge stew of assorted egos. When one is young and callow, one can easily make the mistake of rummaging through the address book, choosing about eight names and trotting to the telephone. Be warned. This way lies disaster. I suppose it may be okay if you are operating an opium den and anticipating that most people will be unconscious within 15 minutes of meeting one another. But if you have a hope of conversation that will last beyond the first sip of wine, it is generally a good idea to invest some thought into the mix of people at the party.

Mixing personalities is much like mixing a fine cocktail. A bit of that, a drop of this, not too much bitterness, a froth of laughter. An icy bit of elegance to balance the rest. Only slight stirring, no shaking, thank you very much. And a lingering taste that becomes a fond memory.

I speak as if I am an expert. I am not. I am a fool who has invited every sort of disastrous personality combination to parties. I once opened my front door to discover a Greenpeace activist and a woman wearing a floor-length fur coat (real dead animal — I swear I could almost smell it) standing next to each other in grim silence. I am still doing penance with my lawyer for the time the ex-cop insulted him just as I was serving a caved-in ice cream angel cake. My greatest worst moment in this department was the party when one guest disappeared. (See sidebar on the following page.)

So, as you can see, I have experience. Bitter, humiliating experience. And if, after that dinner party, I still have the courage to entertain, any idiot can. Forge on. Take heart. Set that table and damn the torpedoes. Every time you falter, think of that evening and become inspired.

This is what I have learned. Blend your dinner guests in your mind as you would a fine recipe, mixing, testing, refining. One can't experiment with people as one does with food and then throw the whole mess in the garbage (much as one would like to on occasion). One must use the imagination. For example, friend Tom is a brilliant scientist. Try to imagine him talking to friend Elaine,

"The woman who says to herself, 'I simply must do something for all the people who have had me to their houses. I'll give a dinner,' and then proceeds to entertain with one fell swoop every one whose courtesy she would like to repay, is doomed to failure before she begins. There is not a chance in the world that the Browns and Greens and Whites, not to speak of the Smiths and Joneses and Harrisons, will make a happy combination of dinner guests."

MARGERY WILSON,
THE POCKET BOOK OF
ETIQUETTE (1937)

the disappearing guest

In our quiet neighbourhood, the Night of the Bathroom Window is legendary.

Just before dessert, a guest vacated the dining room and was never heard from again. I'm not kidding. He went to the bathroom and never came back.

After a while, the remainder of the assembly (not a large group but, until that moment, a jolly gathering) became somewhat concerned about his welfare.

We knocked on the bathroom door. Nothing. We knocked again. More nothing. Then rustlings, clunkings, and ominous noises.

What could he be doing in there?

A terrible thought flashed through my mind: What if he was trying to hang himself from the shower curtain rod with my grandmother's long linen guest towels (which I had spent half an hour ironing, dang!) just to avoid returning to the dinner table?

As a group, we trudged outside into the warm June evening. Stars twinkled above us. In the dark of the bushes that line my property, we could barely find our way around the side of the house, but finally arrived at our destination to discover The Awful Truth. We gazed up at the gaping bathroom window, one and a half storeys above us, and realized that the missing guest had pried open the window, squeezed himself through (and I should note, perhaps unkindly, that he wasn't exactly petite in the derrière department), fallen to the ground, climbed over the five foot high wooden fence, and run off into the night.

Unfortunately, he had also left the bathroom door locked. From the inside.

This meant that somebody had to climb the side of the house, haul herself through the window, and unlock the door. That duty inevitably fell to me, as hostess, despite the fact that nowhere in any of my books on entertaining was there an index item on Climbing Into Bathroom Windows. (There was also a marked absence of volunteers from the assembly.)

I got a leg up from one guest, scrambled onto the shoulders of the tallest man in the crowd, who squealed inelegantly when I finally stood on his head to reach the window, and pulled myself up to straddle the windowsill.

Did I mention I am afraid of heights? I looked down. On my left were the remnants of my dinner guests, staring up at me in awestruck silence. The dog next door started to bark non-stop. On my right was the darkened bathroom. I managed to contort and swing myself into the room, putting one foot down gracefully on the toilet seat to break my fall. Unfortunately, this foot went right through the screen window the departing guest had removed, and which the departing guest had placed on top of the toilet, and then that foot went right into the toilet, which the departing guest had neglected to cover in his haste.

I dried the foot, opened the door, called people inside, and we resumed dinner — and never spoke of him again.

who disdains all science and has just returned from a cult in India. Maybe it could work. But maybe ... you should just shift around a few ingredients. What about Stanley? He is a lawyer, very gentle, always interested in new ideas. Hmmmm. Potential conversation with Elaine. And maybe he could advise her on how to get away from those guys in orange robes who are stalking her ...

Keep imagining the shortlist of the guests talking to one another. As soon as a trouble area looms, shift the ingredients. Keep going. Try every permutation until you think you might have a harmonious blend of personalities who will delight in one another's conversation.

Unbelievable as it may sound, despite my horrifying track record as a cook, the most consistent comment I get after my parties is "That is the best time I have had in a long, long time." People stay late. They talk, and linger over coffee, and laugh gently. They say it's because I invite such great people and make them feel welcome. I think it is because they know that no matter what mind-boggling shockers may land on the table with a curse from the cook, there will be no nasty surprises around the table. They know there will be no sarcasm lurking in the salad, no put-down humour, no meanness, no crotchety criticism, no scoffing or jeering among the people I have invited. This is because I take exquisite care with the guest list, the sort of care some people might say I should have invested in a few cooking classes.

A one-off dinner guest list is an audition for a place on the long-term guest list. If the first time you invite somebody, they misbehave, put them on the back burner. I once invited a woman to an evening of dinner and conversation who, to my horror, did not allow anybody to finish a sentence. I didn't serve fish, but that was unnecessary — the evening consisted of viewing the mouths of my guests gaping like fish as they were cut off mid-comment. I don't like having my sentences finished for me at any time, but especially not when I have just suffered and anguished and screamed and wept in the kitchen for five hours in order to get a meal on the table.

THE QUEST FOR THE PERFECT GUEST

There are myriad potential dinner guests out there. Your challenge is to identify those who are charming, considerate, prompt, generous, and (in my case) have fairly low standards when it comes to food. These are the people who look as if they are entranced by every trivial word emitted by those around them, the ones who chuckle at every gentle joke, who nod in approval at bons mots and tender confessions, who smile and invite and respond in conversation. In other words, the Good Listeners.

I advise you to cultivate these Good Listeners. They are a dying breed, but once you identify and corner one, take all care to preserve the specimen. And invite it to dinner parties, because a Good Listener will save many a disastrous evening.

I must, of course, advise further that a party composed only of Good Listeners will be in danger of falling into silence. Therefore, one must also invite a few Talkers. But for goodness' sake, try to invite Talkers who not only have something to say, and who can say it in an entertaining and concise way, but who also have the good sense and the good manners to know when to stop talking.

This, too, is a lost art. I have a faint suspicion that, on rare occasions, under the influence of stress or chardonnay, I myself may have forgotten the virtues of this lost art. I am now exquisitely aware of exactly how much and how long and how endlessly I am able to prattle without some prudent editing or — better yet — a hook in the wings.

To listen well to others, to express a genuine interest in their conversation, or, even more valiantly, to pretend an interest in their conversation are special talents in our harried world. Between shouting into cell phones while in line at the supermarket, whipping off a dozen e-mails in five minutes, and multitasking as if it were an Olympic event, our daily lives have become overloaded with noise and meaningless interaction.

"At a dinner party, one should eat wisely but not too well, and talk well but not too wisely."

W. SOMERSET MAUGHAM,
A WRITER'S NOTEBOOK (1896)

So many of us become dulled and desensitized to not only the needs of others, but to the simple courtesies of conversation. If I am interrupted in the middle of every sentence, I spend the evening feeling frustrated and unappreciated. Yet the other person, if they are sufficiently self-involved, has the impression that a good time was had by all. I have had too many of these evenings in my life, and I have only so many more left in me. Hence my concern about choosing well my friends and guests. To be in the company of a person who truly listens is a gift: a gift that costs nothing and can be shared. It is also a gift that must not be abused.

CASTING

Personal charms aside, one is known by the company one keeps. If I invite somebody who is rude and sarcastic, my guests will consciously, or subconsciously, make assumptions about my sensibility. Nobody likes to spend an evening being ridiculed or derided. We see others being unspeakably rude, and in our genteel

"In a week or two, one generally forgets just what food was eaten at a certain dinner — but if the guests were all amiable and pleasing, the memory of conversation with them will linger and be constantly associated with the hostess and her home. Many a hostess would be happier (and her guests, too) if less time were paid to the planning of a menu, and more time spent in choosing guests who will be happy together."

LILLIAN EICHLER,
BOOK OF ETIQUETTE (1921)

Canadian way, we don't know what to do about it. So we look the other way, stare at the ceiling, laugh apologetically, as if the rude comments were a great joke, and try to make ourselves invisible. It's the Canadian way.

As I get slightly older and wiser, I see two solutions: don't invite anybody whose behaviour in the past has been suspect, and don't be afraid to show really offensive people the door. I have shown people the door in the past and thoroughly enjoyed it — it is not an admired trait in a hostess, but, at the time, it was justified. I should note that people have to behave really badly for this Rebel Cook to show them the door. (For example, if they spit on the floor, get ill into my favourite vase, hit another guest with the teapot, chase me around the table with the carving knife, or talk politics.)

The dinner table should be a place of sanctuary and harmony. Whether attended by acquaintances or dear friends, it is a time for conviviality and intellectual interaction. It is an opportunity to share thoughts and laughter with others. A dinner party is an occasion and we should all be on our best behaviour.

When choosing guests, anxiety can paralyze the little hostess into indecision. What if I invite a serial killer by mistake? What if Jack and Jill are ex-lovers carrying a grudge and will start to duel with drumsticks? What if Jack and Joe are ex-lovers and are going to retreat into the closet and fight it out? What if Jack, Joe, and Jill are an ex-trio and do not speak to one another throughout the entire meal? (Or worse, what if they do?)

That's the problem with class and discretion. If people don't have the courtesy and consideration to blab vulgarly about their personal life, especially their sex life, how is the little hostess to know what land mines are planted in the guest list? A badly planned dinner can be a culinary thriller. Who knows what secret passions, jealousies, and vendettas lie beneath the surface?

I once attended a dinner where one of the guests, for reasons unknown to me, decided she hated me and my every utterance with the ferocity of the bad witch in *The Wizard of Oz*. She stalked me throughout the night (for it was a stand-up buffet), mocking my every word. If I had been the hostess, I would have jogged into my den and neatly crossed this woman's name off any future guest lists, using a heavy, indelible, permanent marker, the type that is 99¢ at Staples and is very useful

> *"In inviting 'a few friends,' which means a small select company, endeavor to assort them suitably, so as not to bring together people who have no community of tastes feelings, and ideas."*
>
> MISS ELIZA LESLIE,
> *THE BEHAVIOR BOOK:*
> *A MANUAL FOR LADIES* (1853)

for ensuring you don't inflict any more harm on yourself or other innocent bystanders by making the same mistake twice.

So. There you are, with a nice thick pad of paper, designed with pretty flowers (you might want to run out to the dollar store to choose Just the Right One, so the mood is right) and Just the Right Pen. I prefer a Sheaffer fountain pen that is nice and thick and flowing, so that each name looks bee-yoo-tee-full on the page. And just as bee-yoo-tee-full when you cross it out. And even more bee-yoo-tee-full when you write it again ... and so on.

You also need a lovely glass of smooth and rich chardonnay, or perhaps a delicately spicy shiraz. Tinhorn Creek chardonnay (an astoundingly good Canadian wine from British Columbia) or McWilliams Hanwood (a glorious, modestly priced import from Australia) puts me in just the right mood to stare serenely into space while contemplating people and personalities. A large tin of candied pecans are also conducive to deep and important thoughts about the guest list. Munching and sipping is very soothing and helpful to the creative process.

As you are constructing your guest list, you have a

golden opportunity. You can audition the music with which you will entrance the victims/guests. Mellow tenor sax or gentle bossa nova lulls me into a warm, serene, open-minded state as I settle into my chair, staring into space ... zzzzzz ... where was I ... oh, right ... the guest list.

Sit with your glass of whatever (and it doesn't have to be alcoholic; it could be green tea — although, personally, every time I sip green tea, my next five hours are spent in the emergency room chatting with people who have accidentally got their foot stuck in a vise) and imagine who would be "right" around your table.

You do not want people who are loud, unpleasant, or pontificating bores. You especially do not want people who will show up with uninvited children and pets. Don't get me wrong: children are lovely things and are very handy once you are elderly. Parents, of course, generally always think their children are adorable and don't see any reason why their presence at an elegantly set table for eight should be an inconvenience. But their tiny presence at a dinner party can become a stone in the shoe. Unless these children are exquisitely polite (I have met only one, and her name is Annabelle), the guests will flee. Some people, of course, will be insistent

"17 June 1293 ... There came to dinner John of Brabant, with 30 horses and 24 valets at wages, and the two sons of Lord Edmund, with 30 horses and 21 valets, and they stay at our expense in all things, in hay, oats and wages."

HOUSEHOLD ACCOUNTS OF JOHN OF BRABANT AS QUOTED IN *THE NIGHT 2000 MEN CAME TO DINNER AND OTHER APPETIZING ANECDOTES*, EDITED BY DOUGLAS G. MELDRUM

that they bring their tiny heirs, and you should e-mail them the names of several reputable baby-sitting services and then immediately pull out your big black felt pen and cross their names off your list.

So take care that the invitation is either for a single person, or for a single person and a companion, or for a known couple. But no doggies or babies. I once opened the door to find a dinner guest with large pink rollers in her hair. In her arms was a very cute, very active poodle that proceeded to jump over all chairs and sofas, finally settling with its very cute (but probably not very clean) derrière on my very favourite pillow on which to rest my weary head after a fatiguing crossword puzzle. My very favourite pillow, which went straight to the garbage.

There are some professions that will sit most appealingly around your dinner table. I am personally quite fond of lawyers. In my experience, they are the most delightful of dinner guests. I have never had much luck with wrestlers and bikers, but then, maybe they feel the same way about me.

Always invite writers. As a writer myself, I offer these general observations with a total lack of modesty. Writers have ideas and express them well and wittily, but are also willing to listen to others. Writers are Good Listeners (mostly because their minds are whirring — would this make a novel, a screenplay, a poem?). Writers get better with every glass of wine. Unless they are depressed, in which case, hide the bottle.

Exercise caution when inviting actors. As an actor myself, I offer these general observations with affection. Actors can be very funny and love to laugh. Actors appreciate good food and drink. Actors will also stay till dawn and drink everybody under the table. Bless them for being good sports and always ready to rock-and-roll.

These wee guidelines aside, so much of the plotting of a dinner party is intuitive. However, you have to make sure the old intuition is fine-tuned, as opposed to "I think I'll invite Bob the biker and Hilda the feminist performance artist — what fun!" Although this *could* be fun, maybe in a sitcom, around your dinner table it could be a nice little episode of self-destruction.

I have learned the hard way. I have imposed excruciating evenings on unsuspecting dinner guests. I have suffered through self-inflicted torture as guests have decided to air old grudges at my table. I have run into the kitchen to hide carving knives in the freezer, just in case. I have had guests try to duke it out on the lawn. Worse, I have entertained guests so lethally boring that I fell to my knees as the door closed behind them and kissed the hand of the nearest survivor in gratitude for making it through to the end of the evening, so that I was not alone with the bore. Just to make it clear: This is not the sort of entertaining to which I aspire.

Now I know better. Everybody is vetted carefully. If I could get hold of the phone numbers of their first grade teachers, their ex-lovers, and their therapists, I would check them out in every way to make sure there are no unpleasant surprises.

Surprises are fine. Surprises are good. People are surprising by nature and often delightful in their surprisingness. The sorts of surprises I don't want are the unpleasant ones, like an accountant pulling a knife out at dinner, or a teacher spewing neo-Nazi pronouncements over the carrot soup, or anybody showing up wearing a white sheet with darling little eyeholes in it.

Bear in mind my premise: I suffer in the kitchen, weeping and groaning, kicking innocent cabbages around like soccer balls in order to put on the table something that, in some cases, has been totally inedible. Something that, in normal circumstances, would send people stampeding from the room. Therefore, I absolutely must have around my table terrific guests who will delight one another.

Those of you who are brilliant cooks do not need brilliant guests. The food will do the work. I comfort myself with the thought that if the food is great, perhaps people will be so busy eating that the conversation won't be nearly as wonderful as it is around my table, where people will talk about anything

but the food. It would be wonderful if every one of my dinner guests had just returned from a desert island or monastery, where the fare was so grim that even a five-week-old dried-out chicken that had in been in exile in your oven in darkness and despair looked good. (Yes, I have served such things. And the guests were game and gracious.)

So you construct your guest list, squinting over the rim of your wineglass, trying to remember who among your friends and acquaintances is charming, fun, and won't wear mukluks to dinner. When creating the guest list, try to create just the right mood to visualize all the beautiful personalities around your table. When I imagine inviting my guests, I see them around my table and I love them. I imagine them laughing and talking and being and doing all the sweet things they are and do, and I actually manage to get excited about the

"We crossed seventy leagues of desert with much fatigue: the water was brackish, when there was any. We eat dogs, donkeys, and camels."

NAPOLEON BONAPARTE'S DIARY, AFRICA, FEBRUARY 27, 1799

the measure of a guest

This is something that will save you a lot of grief and elbow grease. Working on the assumption that you are such a totally charming person that you have a huge field of options from which to choose your guest list, this is my advice: never invite anybody taller than you.

Now, this may sound like heightism or some sort of arcane prejudice against tall people, but it is really very practical. And they'll never know. And the Human Rights Commission won't care.

Once you start inviting people of a certain height, you have to start cleaning the top of the refrigerator. And the light fixtures. And all the paintings and prints hanging higher than eye level. If you are a perfectionist, you may even have to clean the door ledges. This is hell. Once you invite a

tall person, it is not a dinner party, it is cleaning purgatory. Just think about how much easier everything will be if you invite shorties.

Trust me, I know. In my youth, I was silly enough to have very tall boyfriends. By the time I dusted everything in the house at their eye level, I was too exhausted to serve dinner, to say nothing of any more intimate and frivolous activity. Invite short people and everybody wins. Let the tall ones hire cleaning people and hang out with their own type. (Exception: It is possible to invite tall people — if they are very myopic.)

Conversely, don't invite anybody too short, for they will be at eye level with the dust bunnies under your furniture. It's a fine balance, but eventually you will learn the right height for guests.

dinner. Not about the cooking, mind you. Never about the cooking. But I can get very excited about the people.

CALL TO ARMS

Now comes the tricky part: the inviting.

In my silly youth, when my idea of a good time was putting my feet up and reading an etiquette book or two, I would send out printed invitations to dinner with a little "RSVP" at the bottom of the card. Although everybody (well, almost everybody) I know is polite and considerate, I discovered — too late — that some people don't have any concept of "RSVP." Do they think it means you view them as a "rock star v.i.p."? I gave up on printed invitations pretty darned quick and resorted to phone.

Then I discovered the greatest invention in the world: e-mail. You can send an e-mail to a group of people suggesting a dinner and, even more importantly, a timeline within which they are requested to respond. Some people say that you should put everybody's name in the header, so that they know who else will attend before accepting. That is just toooo much pressure for the Rebel Cook, having to worry about being slighted because my guest list isn't snazzy enough. My guest lists are always plenty snazzy for me, and so far nobody has thrown up on anybody's shoes. What more could you ask for?

Another advantage of e-mail is that the potential guests have a grace period in which to assess the invitation. How awkward is it to receive a phone call with the question, "Are you busy next weekend?" which is bad manners in that it forces an acceptance of the invitation in an intrusive way. You are forced to hem and haw and finally blurt out, "I may be having brunch with the Queen, but if your invitation is really wonderful, I can take a rain check with the monarch." So e-mail is a buffer, giving people time to organize their thoughts. It also means that the Rebel Cook can construct the invitation in exactly the words she wants and then, with a deep breath, press Send and know she is committed to the adventure.

After I get a few responses, I sometimes drop hints about the other guests. Perhaps I will say "Oh, and Bill and Erin are coming — you met them at that full moon meditation." Or, at the last minute, as I am finalizing and confirming, I may reveal names in an e-mail header, mostly because then it is easier for the guests to remember them later. (One little problem with this last technique is that some people do not want their e-mails spread around like sesame seeds on the Internet loaf, and I don't blame them. My feeling is that if

"Dinner invitations must be answered at once. It is most inconsiderate to leave a hostess in uncertainty and unable to complete her party."

LADY TROUBRIDGE,
THE BOOK OF ETIQUETTE (1926)

there are only half a dozen names on the list, it is not such a sin.)

Every now and again, you will run into a wee snag. Of the eight people you contact, only two are available for the evening in question. (In my case, of course, dialogue may be going on in the other household along the lines of "I would sooner die than eat another piece of petrified chicken at that dame's place — I do not want to have my stomach pumped again!" But I hope not ...)

Sometimes, the universe does not unfold like a beautiful dinner napkin, and it becomes clear that you are not meant to entertain that particular evening. Except, you have some who have declined and two brave souls who have accepted. In that case, you can either invite the people who have accepted to a really intimate, informal dinner, or you can quickly forage for more guests, or you can cut your losses and reschedule. There is some loss of face in this, and it takes delicate manoeuvring not to make the guests who have accepted feel as if an evening with just their company is insufficient. However, most people who have entertained understand that a convivial evening — a dinner party — is an event that requires planning and coordination.

There is always the moment of relief when all have confirmed. Yes! It is going to be a dinner! It is going to happen!

And then ... the terror begins ...

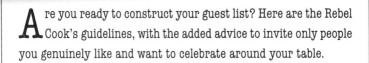

the good and the bad

Are you ready to construct your guest list? Here are the Rebel Cook's guidelines, with the added advice to invite only people you genuinely like and want to celebrate around your table.

Good Guests

- People who know how to talk — but not too much
- People who know how to eat — but whose standards are low
- People who know how to drink — and who will bring extra bottles — and designated drivers
- Good listeners
- Kind people
- Short people

Bad Guests

- People who arrive early, way early
- People who bring bundles of flowers that need to be cut and arranged on the spot
- Political blowhards
- Women (or men) who wear stiletto heels on your hardwood floors (house depreciation: roughly $100 per step, $200 per stomp)
- Drunken men with chips on their shoulders
- Drunken women with lips on those shoulders

check your weapons
and count your chickens

"'Tis burnt, and so is all the meat.
What dogs are these! Where is the rascal cook?
How durst you, villains, bring it from the dresser,
And serve it thus to me that love it not?"

WILLIAM SHAKESPEARE,
THE TAMING OF THE SHREW

I see the kitchen as a battlefield. I shout at the vegetables, threaten the chicken, and engage in continuing hostile dialogues with any character in the recipe that does not do what I want it to do. I think of myself as a spiritual sort of gal, but not, alas, when I am cooking. I am trying to reform, especially after being told off roundly for my sins by a real cook when I told him of my recent fight with a cabbage.

"You have to love the cabbage! You have to love the food and dominate it!" he cried. What a concept. Sitting quietly in the kitchen, seducing the cabbage before cooking it. I think that gets me too close to the cabbage. You see, once I actually bond with the cabbage, how will I chop it and cook it and eat it? I have had problems with pumpkins to which I have become too attached, and I don't want to start with cabbages, squashes, melons, and sides of spare ribs, or I really won't be able to cook anything ever. I will either subsist on 52-Additives Cereal or have to take up plumbing so I can afford to dine out at expensive restaurants, where my only connection to the food will be the head waiter.

Cooking, in particular, is something that, years ago, was regarded as a required talent in any woman. Now, many women I know take pride in having no knowledge of the kitchen. I know a woman who was a defiant non-cook, married a sweet soul who could barely cook, and, as far as I know, they have moved to a cabin in the woods and have starved to death. I also know a couple who married young. She cooked 365 different meals in the first year of their marriage and then threw down the frying pan, like a glove, and never cooked again.

the pumpkin

We should never have become so fond of the pumpkin. When I brought it home from the supermarket, having won it in a draw (one of the few I have ever won), we fussed over it and petted it. It was a prize, after all. I painted a jolly jack-o'-lantern grin on it with felt pen, infusing it with just the right tone of cheerful eagerness. I tied a jaunty ribbon round its stem. We set it on the kitchen table and included it in dinner conversation. We commented frequently on its cuteness, leaning toward it as we did so, letting it know of our approval.

This went on for weeks.

Then, eventually, we began to realize, quietly, separately, that the pumpkin would not be with us forever. We tried not to mention it at first. But then, gradually, one of us would say, with false heartiness, that we would some day have to "you know ...," with eyes rolling back and forth toward The Orangeness at the edge of the kitchen table.

Finally, the day came. I couldn't be there. I had to leave. I couldn't bear to see the knives, the mess, the seeds, the stem ...

We ate it. Our little pet. I still feel guilty.

We should never have become so fond of that pumpkin.

Luckily, he is a brilliant cook. The cliché is "Can she bake a cherry pie?" The reality, for me, is "Can she have people to dinner without killing them?"

Although I would not presume to say I cook anything well, I have managed to ferret out a few chicken recipes that sometimes (oh, okay, maybe once in a blue moon) turn out all right. The original recipes are incredibly ornate, and trust me, after trying once or twice, I quickly abandoned any futile hope of cooking the originals without turning into a hopeless drunk or running away to an ashram, where I would never have to cook chicken again. I pruned (maybe smashed or decimated would be better words) the recipes down to the bare minimum.

"This was a good dinner enough, to be sure: but it was not a dinner to ask a man to."

SAMUEL JOHNSON

I know this is sacrilege to the purist, but I am a desperate woman. I am determined to entertain with the gallantry of one doomed to failure (think Scarlett O'Hara in her mother's green velvet drapes), and I will gamely use whatever weapons are available. I use enough weird ingredients that the hapless guests tend to think the dishes are far more complicated than they really are.

And while I am hesitant to give any advice whatsoever in the kitchen, I see a relationship between creative

43

> *"Cooking is like love. It should be entered into with wild abandon or not at all."*
>
> HARRIET VAN HORNE

courage and kitchen courage. As an artist reaches the point of throwing aside fear and simply leaping into the work with joy and courage, and with that confidence finds their voice and their way of reaching others with their talent, so a cook may do the same. I hasten to add that I do not count myself among those who are artists in the kitchen. But, in my limited way, I have found that if I throw aside inhibitions, preconceived notions, and fear of cooking, I can, on occasion, create a dish or a meal that is perfectly okay. Maybe even better than okay.

First, you need to know the turf of the battlefield, the history, what skirmishes and successful campaigns have transpired in the past. For this vital research, buy a handful (or more) of well-written books about food and cooking. You will forget about all the horrible challenges of measuring cups and thermometers and revel in good writing. Then the recipes will come as little decorations on the cake.

M. F. K. Fisher introduced me to the culture of food. Her straightforward, detailed, and loving descriptions of meals and occasions changed my perception of the dinner. In her works (*How to Cook a Wolf, Consider the Oyster, Serve It Forth, The Gastronomical Me,* and *An Alphabet for Gourmets,* brought together in a compen-

44

dium called *The Art of Eating*), she takes you, the passenger, on a journey through food and cooking, told in simple yet elegant style. Fisher is the icon, the standard held so high above the heads of the rest of us that she complains of a dearth of dinner invitations, as most people were too intimidated to cook for her. (I have never had that problem.)

Peg Bracken's *The I Hate to Cook Book* is at the opposite end of the spectrum, full of just the sort of sneaky little tricks I need to know. I roared through the recipes in her book and actually managed to make a few. And nobody died. She is my kind of gal. Throw the food in a pot, pour a glass of something delicious, fall onto the sofa, and let the chips fall where they may. Her recipes fit her philosophy: much better to laugh and snooze than to slave

"In the kitchen, next to courage, the hand and the eye are the most important assets. Neatness counts, in cooking as in everything else. You need be neither witty nor handsome to produce a great soufflé, but your fingers must have that innate knowledge of just how things should feel."

GEORGE BRADSHAW, *SUPPERS AND MIDNIGHT SNACKS*

in the kitchen for naught. You have to love somebody who includes recipes such as Old Faithful and Stayabed Stew. If you are even a fraction as incompetent in the kitchen as I am, you will find this book a treasure trove of crafty little tips and ploys.

If you can find a writer who pleases you, you have

taken a great leap as a Rebel Cook. Browse through books at libraries and bookstores and choose one that speaks to you. Once you are inspired by a thought or an image that excites you about that once-grim prospect of cooking, you have made a breakthrough: the notion that you might actually enjoy preparing a meal. Hard to fathom, but it could happen.

The Rebel Strategy

So. You have been incredibly brave and invited four or five people to dinner. This is a good beginning. Start with a manageable number. (To be really safe, you might start with you and your dog. Do the whole candlelit table routine and see how he/she reacts.)

Now you have to choose a menu. There are standbys: chili and spaghetti. I have never cooked either of these in my life. So if that is what you are looking for, put down this book, go out and buy a case of beer and a pizza, rent an action flick, and call a bunch of your friends. Have a good time. Invite me too. It means I would not have to cook.

Nevertheless, despite my jibes, a good chili or spaghetti is delightful for the courage of its simplicity. One of the most wonderful meals I ever had was on an arctic winter night some years ago, when a gentleman friend cooked up a redolent spaghetti sauce with an al dente pasta, accompanied by a simple green salad. Four of us drank red wine, ate with resounding appetite, and played mah-jong into the wee hours of the night. This gentleman had a wonderful advantage: he could cook. Perhaps this was the only thing he could cook. I will never find out. Alas, we parted ways shortly afterward. But I do know that if this meal is the only thing he ever learned to cook, it will stand him in good stead for the next 30 years. He is now sort of famous, in a modest Canadian way, and every time I see him on television, I think of that fabulous spaghetti dinner.

This sentimental example (the sentiment is for the spaghetti, not the gentleman, however nice he was) has a basic lesson hidden in its memories. If you can cook one thing well, bravo! You have a staple, a fallback position, a weapon in your hands with which you can brave the world of entertaining. Even if you serve this same meal again and again to the same people, worrying that they might collapse of ennui on your table, my guess is that as long as you create an atmosphere in which they can enjoy themselves, they won't care. And they know they won't die.

I have heard of couples who were great successes at

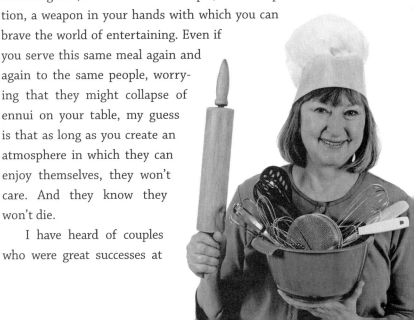

entertaining, yet they cooked only one meal all year long. They invited people again and again for the same meal, changing the menu annually. I like that sort of attitude. If you find something that works, don't tinker.

You have several choices: stick to the basics and hope for the best, gallop into unknown territory and hope to confound them, or draw them in as confederates and ask for their support. The last is the coward's way, but it serves the very noble purpose of drawing out your guests and making them feel useful once you have revealed yourself as incompetent. I frequently ask some hapless guest to test the chicken for doneness, since I am Never Really Sure. This not only makes them feel very useful and important, but it also casts a healthy pall of uncertainty on the meal. If the hostess is worried, shouldn't they be worried as well? I always hope this will be a useful ploy in future lawsuits, hoping I am suddenly on firmer ground if I have implicitly warned them about my cooking.

Sometimes sticking to the basics is a brilliant strategy, and the simplest recipes can often be your entrée into the world of successful entertaining. One of the most unusual dinner parties I ever attended consisted of one course: cabbage soup. It sounds dreadful, but it was delicious. And a good time was had by all.

One of my mother's great triumphs in the kitchen was the night a horde of guests arrived unexpectedly.

All she had was three pheasants. She cooked the birds slowly in tomato, green pepper, and garlic (known as a *pörkölt* to Hungarians), and 20 years later, people were still rhapsodizing about her pheasant dinner. To this day, she remains astounded by this.

Or experiment: be wild, creative, throw something on the table that your innocent guests have never seen or dreamed existed. Keep them on their toes. If they don't know what they are eating, how are they to pass judgment on your cooking? In my foolish youth, I acquired a rather musty book on French cookery. It was falling apart. It smelled. But it was intriguing. Insane as it sounds, I actually tried to make some of the recipes.

One in particular was so totally beyond the norm of dining in my circles that my eyes whizzed around like Frisbees the moment I saw it. Yes! Weird, wonderful, and with a pedigree! As the cookbook is long gone, disintegrated or perhaps ground and served for dinner in a distracted moment, all I can remember is that it required little bits of lamb wrapped with vegetables in foil and served with great style. I presented this on several occasions, and my guests gave every indication of enjoying it immensely. It may have helped that dinner was two hours late. The downside was that I misread the

> "*Murder is commoner among cooks than among members of any other profession.*"
>
> W. H. AUDEN

recipe and four grown-ups had to make do with servings that had shrunk to the size of a Ping-Pong ball. But give me points for effort. Those guests had never had such a thing before and (mercifully) will no doubt ever experience it again.

Don't forget your ethnicity. The meals your momma served you may seem ordinary to you, but to people of a different culture, those same menus may be exciting and exotic. I have had great luck raiding the Hungarian recipe books of my family. I know a good scam when I find one.

I say this as a desperate Rebel Cook. I will fling the wildest concoctions on the table, then go to the kitchen to pray. However, having said that, I am also hopeful, knowing that I have invited interesting, kind, and intelligent people to my table, people who will greet any shortcoming with forgiveness and good cheer. One of the most perfect guests I have hosted once said, when I apologetically handed her a drink in an inadequate, short, and dowdy wineglass, "Oh, my dear, long stems are such an affectation."

MIND YOUR MENU

Yes, after all the weeping and carrying on, after plying the guests with endless drink, there comes the moment of truth. You must go into the kitchen and return with something edible.

This generally means recipes have come into play at some point — ideally, well before the day of the dinner. And so we must gird our loins, count our chickens (and hope they don't squawk in terror, leap out of the pan, and run from the kitchen), and say our prayers.

Under no circumstances should you plan a dinner party without planning the menu, unless you are operating under such a haze of opiates, booze, or ego that you just don't care. (If this is the case, this is my advice: maybe you shouldn't be entertaining. Maybe you should be checking into a rehab centre, seeing a nice holistic therapist, or booking a session with the Dalai Lama.) A recipe is like homework. It is a duty, it initially seems boring, but it gets you a passing grade, and, if you are lucky, it opens your eyes to more experiences.

I have never met a recipe that doesn't make me blanch and clutch the table. Even the simple ones, the ones that seduce me into thinking, "Oh, this is easy, I could make this." There is always a catch. Always some little trick that everybody in the world but me knows about. For the Rebel Cook and her

hail caesar

Most people invited to dinner expect a salad, which I find exhausting to make. Cutting up all those leaves of lettuce into artful little pieces takes way too much of one's precious prime-time years. I subscribe to the theory that guests should be grateful that I washed the green stuff and hacked off the brown bits. Then I throw it into a bowl and toss a few nuts and seeds on top (after ascertaining that no guest is allergic to nuts or seeds, in which case the assembly would adjourn to the emergency ward for the rest of the evening — this is why it is a good idea to ask about food allergies).

Bear in mind this is not a recipe. This is a fallback position for those of us who are not gifted in the salad or salad dressing department. I am so hopeless with salad dressing that one set of guests took to bringing along their own special concoction as self-defence against my incompetence. My only success, left to my own evil designs, was adding a jar of marinated artichokes, which most people seemed to like. (Or at least, maybe they liked it better than a bare naked salad.)

I love Caesar salad and have tried more than 25 times to make a decent Caesar salad dressing. And I have failed more than 25 times — until I finally found a recipe for a good Caesar salad dressing that I am eager to share.

The Rebel Cook's Caesar Salad

- Wash hands.
- Wash romaine lettuce. Put in bowl.
- Wash hands again.
- Get in car.
- Drive to supermarket.
- Walk to aisle that says "Vegetable oil, vinegar," turning up nose in defiance.
- Walk past that section to the section that says "Salad dressing."
- Choose salad dressing.
- Pay.
- Drive home.
- Wash hands.
- Pour on salad, and give it a shake to show it who's boss.
- Collapse in chair and congratulate oneself on job well done.

compatriots, this is a constant. Why do so many cookbooks assume you know the basics, like how to measure butter or milk or water or kumquats? Not everybody learned this in finishing school.

Generally, I spend so long looking for a recipe that after a while I just want to go to bed with a bowl of candied pecans and a nice shiraz. I am amazed, confounded, stricken dumb when I see the recipes in *Martha Stewart Living* and *Gourmet*. Who has time to make that stuff? Who eats that stuff? I read one page of those glorious recipes, and although I look at them dreamily (as one who collects cookbooks just for the joy of never having to cook what is within) and sometimes even tear them out in a masochistic way, I feel faint at the thought of trying to assemble and serve any such dish. I just know there will be something in there to trip me up, a nice little banana peel for the innocent in the kitchen. Besides, I would rather be sitting with my feet up, sipping something lovely, and reading a food magazine anyway.

I was once gifted (rather pointedly) with a copy of *The Joy of Cooking* by a friend who had served me dinner way too many times. Years later, my kitchen is littered with cookbooks, most of them arcane and delightful, and only a few of them practical. I love cookbooks. I love recipes. I love drooling over the pictures, the ingredients, making careful notes about ingredients, imagining the glorious serving of the finished product. I daydream, I plan, I map my shopping route, I work myself into a frenzy of anticipation, and then I reach the peak of excitement and throw down the cookbook with a cackle of joy. Because I am not planning to cook any of it! Is this a great life or what?

"No one who cooks cooks alone. Even at her most solitary, a cook in the kitchen is surrounded by generations of cooks past, the advice and menus of cooks present, the wisdom of cookbook writers."

LAURIE COLWIN, AS QUOTED IN *SIMPLE ABUNDANCE: A DAYBOOK OF COMFORT AND JOY,* BY SARAH BAN BREATHNACH

I have a weakness for unusual and dainty cookbooks, tomes about Victorian tea, Depression-era recipes, theme cookbooks, in fact, any cookbook that looks a little unusual and eccentric. The older and the mustier, the more I enjoy it. I love opening a cookbook that may be 50 to 100 years old and wondering about the other hands that touched those pages, the meals that were made, the families that were brought together by the recipes within.

Sentiment and history aside, cookbooks, in all their diversity, are valuable to you, the Rebel Cook, for another reason. If you are discouraged, desperate, and wonder how on earth you will ever be able to entertain ... and if, even worse, you are totally without enthusiasm for the prospect of cooking a meal for yourself, to say nothing of guests, a browse through a cookbook may be a tonic for your weakened spirit.

Like Charlie Brown, I am forever filled with hope that the football will not be snatched away at the last moment. On second thought, perhaps the football allusion is not the best choice. I once served a chicken that looked somewhat like a deflated football. I don't feel quite so bad when I remind myself that one of my friends once baked dinner buns so concrete in composition that a guest took one outside and ran over it with his truck as an experiment. The bun was unscathed. The tires will never be the same. I find this inspiring. The sort of story that keeps me cooking.

I am also inspired (when I am not totally cowed) by the truly gifted. I once attended a gourmet dinner and wine-tasting at which a velvety Tinhorn Creek merlot was served with a roasted chestnut soup so extraordinary that a sensual hush fell over the room, followed moments later by a spontaneous round of applause for the cook. This soup was such a transforming experience to my taste buds that I decided to transform myself as a cook, as well. I was determined to make this soup, an ambition that, in retrospect, is somewhat like Little Lulu trying to climb Mount Everest with nothing but

Tubby's skipping rope for support. Luckily, I knew the chef, Gail Norton of the Cookbook Co. Cooks, and she shared her recipe. As she is painfully aware of my non-skills in the kitchen, she no doubt hung up the phone and lay down on the floor and laughed so hard all her pots and pans fell off the wall.

Her recipe is exquisite. A recipe for gourmets and gourmands. But not for a gourl like me, whose eyes started to go funny once she hit the cipolline onions and the foie gras. So I cheated. I took the basics — roasted chestnuts, onions, garlic, and Armagnac — and did what I could.

It was darned hard to find chestnuts, but I picked up a big bag of the little cuties at a discount supermarket, congratulating myself at the checkout for how stylish and sophisticated I must appear. (I tend to get lost in any store larger than a deli.)

I started the soup at nine in the evening. By midnight, I was weeping profusely, with bloody bandages adorning eight of my ten digits. Only two had escaped the knife I wielded as I attempted to peel the chestnuts. They slipped, they skewed, they ran around the counter as if they had a mind of their own, the little devils. And of

> "When you hate to cook, a supermarket is an appalling place. You see so many things that they all blur, and you finally end up with a glazed look and a chop."
>
> PEG BRACKEN,
> THE I HATE TO COOK BOOK

course every time they did that, the knife slipped and I nicked another finger.

Every now and again I would take a break and do another Internet search on peeling chestnuts. (Yes, this is indeed a great waste of an hour of the prime years of one's life.) I followed the instructions, each time ending up with another bandage. Since I had hopes of playing the piano again, I finally cried uncle, left the unspeakable mess of chestnut shells, pulp, blood, and tears in the kitchen, and e-mailed Gail, sobbing pitifully as I pecked at the keyboard with my two unbandaged digits, begging for enlightenment.

Her prompt four-word response: "Canned chestnuts, my dear."

Now, I ask you, how is the little cook supposed to cook any meal when there are all these trade secrets nobody ever tells you? My theory is that the real cooks pretend that it is so obvious that any idiot would know it, but really, it is just a ruse to keep the rest of us paralyzed in the kitchen.

Once I knew the Canned Chestnut Secret, I threw all the gloop into the garbage, put fresh bandages on my pinkies, and, the next day, set out in search of canned chestnuts. This took some time, as canned chestnuts are not a staple at most neighbourhood grocery stores in my part of the world. After arguing with a teenaged clerk for some time about the fact that even *I* knew that water chestnuts are not the same as roasted chestnuts, I finally hit the road to various gourmet grocery stores. After maxing out my credit card to get the gold-plated can of chestnuts, I headed home and tried again.

This is the inspiring part: I actually made this soup. And it tasted good. I substituted stuff here and there, but it remains one of my crowning achievements in the kitchen. And next time I have three weeks to spare and MasterCard raises my limit, I might make it for a dinner party.

Gail Norton's Roasted Chestnut Soup Garnished with Grilled Foie Gras

- 16 pearl onions (cipolline onions are great if you can find them)
- olive oil
- 8 pieces crystallized ginger, sliced
- butter
- 5 large shallots, minced
- 2 garlic cloves, minced
- 1 c. (250 mL) roasted chestnuts
- 2 pods star anise
- 6 allspice berries
- 3 sprigs thyme
- ⅓ c. (75 mL) Armagnac
- 6 c. (1.5 L) veal stock
- lobe foie gras

1. Preheat oven to 375°F (190°C). Toss the pearl onions with a bit of olive oil. Roast with their jackets on for 30 to 45 minutes, until they are soft and luscious. Remove from the oven and allow to cool enough that you can handle them. Remove them from their jackets, cut in half, and put in a bowl with the crystallized ginger pieces.

2. Heat a large frying pan and add enough olive oil to just cover the bottom of the pan, add 2 tbsp. (25 mL) butter,

and once the fat is quite hot, add the shallots, cook until slightly soft, then add the garlic cloves. Turn down the heat, add the chestnuts, star anise, allspice berries, and thyme. Put the lid on the pan and allow the mixture to sweat for at least 15 minutes. Do not let the onions brown.

3. Add the Armagnac and reduce slightly, then add the veal stock and simmer gently for at least 30 minutes to allow the chestnuts to thoroughly soften and the flavours to meld.

4. Remove the spices and the thyme from the pot and, using a hand blender or blender, purée to desired thickness — add water if you want to thin the consistency. Return to the pan.

5. Slice the foie gras into pieces at least ¾ in. (2 cm) thick. Season with salt and pepper. Heat a frying pan until very hot (there is no need to add oil to the pan), sear one side until brown, turn over for only a few seconds.

To serve: Add a slice of foie gras to a bowl (make sure you take a bit of the foie gras fat along), top with a ladle of the chestnut soup, and garnish with a spoonful of the roasted onions and ginger. Top with a sprig of thyme.

Serves 6–8

The Rebel Cook's Roasted Chestnut Soup

(Purists, and especially Gail Norton, cover your eyes)

- **olive oil**
- **butter**
- **garlic**
- **cut-up crystallized ginger**
- **any old onion**
- **roasted chestnuts in can, tube, or jar**
- **chicken broth**
- **allspice, clove, nutmeg, or anything that might be a relative**
- **brandy, port, sherry, red wine, or anything alcoholic that is a deep red in colour**

Throw into a pot the olive oil, butter, garlic, ginger, and any sort of onion you can get your hands on. Cook it up until it smells nice. Add a can or tube of roasted chestnuts. Stir, and smell. Pour yourself a glass of something to while away the time while stirring. After a few minutes, add a can of chicken broth and anything in your spice drawer that is close to allspice. (I have tried nutmeg and clove.) Add a splash of the best brandy in your cupboard or, in a pinch, some red wine. After it has cooked a bit, throw it in a blender, put on the top securely, say a little prayer, and give it a good whiz. Then throw it back in the pot, heat it again, and serve.

I swear, although it is nowhere nearly as good as Gail's, after tasting it, people will fall about deliriously, kiss your hand, and proclaim you a goddess in the kitchen.

Real Simple (The Rebel Cook Gets Sweet)

Every now and again, a recipe will leap out at you. You will love the ingredients, the imagined taste, the presentation, and, more importantly, you may think "I could make that!"

And so you should. Although I have a million ruses, in my little heart of hearts, I recognize the power of simplicity.

In a delightful book called *Plots and Pans,* a wonderful blend of food and Canadian literary trivia and quotes, I found a recipe so simple I was ecstatic. I defy anybody, even me, to make a mess of this.

Gingered Oranges

- **4 juice oranges, each about 8 oz. (250 g)**
- **2 oz. (60 g) fresh ginger**
- **pinch ground cumin (optional)**

1. Peel oranges. Be careful to remove all the white pith and work over a bowl to catch any juice. Cut the oranges into ¼ in. (0.5 cm) slices and remove any seeds. Add the slices to the juice in the bowl.

2. Peel and grate the ginger and add to the oranges and juice.

3. Refrigerate until well chilled. If desired, sprinkle with cumin before serving.

Serves 4

I had never made a successful cake in my cooking campaign until I read the article "Five Easy Pieces" by Kathy Richardier, with simple recipes for fabulous cakes. This changed my life. I no longer have to leap out of my chair just after the main course shouting "I think the furnace is about to blow!" and rush people out of the house. I can now serve dessert.

Although I have since encountered variations of these recipes in other books, I am forever grateful to Ms. Richardier for assembling them in one article, which I have since copied myriad times. The original piece of paper is daubed with oil, butter, and even a few spatters of poppy seed, but I think this adds to its charm. It is folded and creased, and I regularly lose it in the rubble of my recipes (which are like a culinary landfill in which only 10 percent of the goods are actually usable). Then, once every two years, I find the faded, folded article, clutch it to my bosom, and immediately trot to the phone and invite some innocent victims to dinner.

Lemon Poppy Seed Cake

- 1 c. (250 mL) boiling water
- ¼ c. (50 mL) poppy seeds
- 1 Deluxe Duncan Hines lemon cake mix (this is allowable once in a while)
- 1 box lemon instant pudding, 4-portion size
- ½ c. (125 mL) vegetable oil
- 4 eggs

Glaze
- ½ c. (125 mL) sugar
- 4 tbsp. (50 mL) butter
- 5–6 tbsp. (75 mL) lemon juice

1. Preheat oven to 350°F (180°C). Pour poppy seeds and boiling water into a large bowl and let soak for several minutes. Add cake mix, pudding, vegetable oil, and eggs and blend thoroughly. Beat for 2 minutes and pour into a well-greased, lightly floured Bundt pan.

2. Bake about 45 minutes or until a toothpick inserted into the centre comes out clean.

3. To make the glaze, bring ingredients to a boil and cook until sugar dissolves.

4. Let cake cool in pan for 15 minutes, loosen sides with knife, and pour glaze over cake. De-pan the cake when it is completely cool. This cake stores very well for days or even weeks.

Serves 4

This cake is so simple that even I don't need the idiot version. It tastes as if you slaved in the kitchen, making everything from scratch. The glaze is the trick. Anything syrupy at the end of a meal will melt even the hardest palate. People will beg for the recipe. I urge you to tell them to buy this book.

Another recipe from the famous "Five Easy Pieces" article is Cynthia Zeger's Chocolate Cake. It is a terribly rich and wonderfully bad-for-you dark chocolate feast. I served this once to a friend (who is a brilliant cook) and she ate the whole thing in one sitting, then demanded the recipe. I was somewhat startled, but flattered.

If you are on a roll, you can play around with other simple cake recipes. I think the very best ones (other than the above) are from the late Laurie Colwin. I loved Laurie Colwin when I read her first words in *Gourmet,* and I loved her spirit even more when I read the collections of her essays on food. Especially when I found a number of recipes that basically translate as "Throw the gunk in a bowl, mix it, and ladle it out into a pan"! That's my language.

You may have noticed that not all of this is good for your health or waistline. Well, excuse me. I am not a cook. I am a demented hostess, and I will settle for anything that is easy to make and noshy. If you want healthy, trot down to your nearest health food store and buy some nice molasses soy bran cookies and serve them to your guests. See how long you last on the social circuit. Two minutes is my guess. And the bathroom window will see a lot of traffic.

FUELLED BY DESPERATION, INSPIRED BY ART

Literature and film abound with fabulous dining scenes. When we see the boorish diner in *Big Night* eating her offensive meatballs with cigarette in hand, we understand the anguish of the chef. When we see Babette create a work of art from her last pennies in order to honour and heal the men and women of her remote Nordic town, it is truly *Babette's Feast*.

"He made for the cellar door, and presently reappeared, somewhat dusty, with a bottle of beer in each paw and another under each arm. 'Self-indulgent beggar you seem to be, Mole,' he observed. 'Deny yourself nothing. This is really the jolliest little place I ever was in. Now, wherever did you pick up those prints?'"

KENNETH GRAHAME,
THE WIND IN THE WILLOWS

When we read *The Wind in the Willows* and see the care with which Rattie hosts his friends, it is the notion of hospitality, not of abundance, that touches our heart. As Mole frets and worries about his meagre staples, as he tries to host Rat in turn, the kindness and graciousness of Rat is an example of how we all should behave in the moment of guest and host.

I frequently feel like Mole, trying desperately to

"Cooks are in some ways very much like actors; they must be fit and strong, since acting and cooking are two of the most exacting professions. They must be blessed — or cursed, whichever way you care to look at it — with what is called the artistic temperament, which means that if they are to act or cook at all well, it cannot be for duds or dummies."

ANDRÉ SIMON,
THE CONCISE ENCYCLOPEDIA
OF GASTRONOMY (1952)

create a memorable evening from nothing. Or like Alice in Wonderland, seeing bizarre dishes that I don't remember cooking land on the table.

This is my theory: take a fancy, intricate recipe with a name that would intimidate even Emeril (something like "A Baroque Feast for Seven Drunken Fiddlers Prepared in the Inuit Style"), a recipe that has maybe 79 ingredients. Then, sneakily, craftily, choose at random any 10 of these ingredients (five if you are really feeling rebellious), fling them together, serve it to the guests, and call it "A Contemporary Feast for Seven Drunken Fiddlers Prepared in the [insert your name here] Style." I ask you — is anybody going to argue with you?

Contemplate this scenario: one has invited people to dinner. One sits and anguishes, with three or four scotches, over what to serve. One knows that if the incompetent cook serves something familiar, in the ken of the guests, they will know immediately the failure of the dish. The Rebel Cook must ferret out a recipe that is so arcane, so weird, so ethnic, so beyond the norm that nobody at the table will have a clue. (Which puts them on equal standing with the Cook.)

I have found such recipes. They are daunting. They are breathtaking. They are horrific. But oh ho ho! They are an escape route from the certain public humiliation that awaits me if I were to serve, say, pot roast. A useful ploy is to find a complicated recipe that reflects your ethnicity, so that, if challenged, you can say reverently, "Oh, this was my great-grandmother's specialty, passed down through the generations until it found its way into my kitchen." It is important to say this with a straight face.

Here's what I mean: let us revel in the maze of Esterhazy Rostelyos, pronounced, as far as I can tell, Esther-HAH!-zee RAOSH-tell-yosh. In his excellent book *The Cuisine of Hungary,* George Lang presents a recipe for this dish that is as beautifully crafted and ornate as a fine piece of heirloom embroidery, no doubt an inspiration and mecca to those who read it. This recipe turns up in almost every Hungarian cookbook in some form, always with 17 million ingredients and just as many steps. I am not going to reprint it here, because if you are talented enough to make the original recipe, you sure don't need this book, and you maybe should be consider working as a chef at the Four Seasons or Ritz-Carlton.

After working my way through a wide range of cookbooks, all intimidating, I finally found a tiny cookbook the size of a health care laboratory pamphlet (the sort you pick up at pharmacies to kill time while waiting for your typhoid prescription). It is optimistically (given its modest size) titled *The Hungarian Cookbook* and was published by the Culinary Arts Institute in 1954. In it is a rendition of Esterhazy Rostelyos that can be scanned in less than five minutes and that has fewer than 55 ingredients.

This is promising. The Rebel Cook is encouraged. George Lang's version is the aristocrat of recipes, the gourmet version, the sort that moneyed people in penthouses ask their cooks (who are paid astounding sums of money by Rebel Cook standards) to whip up. It is also the version that foodies, chefs, and people who are naturally talented in the kitchen will no doubt not bat an eye at. But, to the humble kitchen klutz, it is formidable. Then there is the version that is slightly less complicated but still beyond the reach of the Rebel Cook. This is when the Rebel Cook takes a deep breath and plunges into dangerous waters. (Any real cook reading this would be well advised to put down this book right now and take a jog around the block, for they may become faint at the sacrilege I am about to advise.)

Knowing how hopeless I am in the kitchen, when

I look at a recipe, I ascertain what is possible given my resources and limited skills. So. I have in my hands two versions of an elegant, interesting recipe, neither of which will I be able to pull off with any degree of success. The original recipes call for beef, but red meat always turns to leather on my stove. At least with chicken, I know I have a 50/50 — oh, okay, 30/70 — chance of success. So this is what I did. You may choose a different approach. It is your kitchen, after all.

("Chicken" in Hungarian is *csirke,* just so you aren't confused. A recipe for *Esterhazy Kupecsirke* is on the next page.)

Amazingly, people claim to love this dish. I challenge you to look at the recipe, come up with your own variation, and embellish it with a personal moniker. If you have a lot of bravura, you can even try to pass yourself off as one of the Esterhazy descendants, rhapsodizing about how this aristocratic recipe found its way in to your loving hands.

Yet another mutation of an elegant recipe is a simple Hungarian version of chicken and rice. (See the recipe on page 74.) If I can cook it, anybody can. If you want to waste the prime years of your life cutting up a chicken, go ahead; otherwise, buy some chicken thighs or chicken breasts (and cut them up into little pieces if you wish — I'd rather sit with my feet up reading a fashion magazine).

Esterhazy Kupecsirke

- **enough chicken to feed three or four people**
- **3 carrots**
- **2 stalks celery**
- **1 onion**
- **1 parsnip**
- **salt, pepper**
- **capers (if you are feeling rich and if you hit the right store at the right time)**
- **white wine (if you are drinking it)**
- **sour cream or yogurt**
- **paprika**

Fling the chicken into a skillet and brown it. No holds barred. Put it onto a plate, and then brown the carrots, celery, onion, parsnip, and salt and pepper. Add some broth if you have any. Throw the chicken back into the skillet and don't be too precious about it. Throw in the capers if you remembered to buy them. Cook some more. Add a splash of white wine (maybe the stuff left over from your last dinner party).

Keep it cooking while you sit with a nice glass of port and listen to Billie Holiday singing "Gloomy Sunday," one of those jolly Hungarian songs that was reportedly banned in Hungary at one time because Hungarians were throwing themselves in the Danube in despair every time they heard it. It's a Hungarian thing. Lift up the lid, see how the chicken is doing. If it doesn't squawk, it must be nearly done. Add some sour cream and paprika and let it heat some more. Spoon it onto big plates with salad and a crusty loaf on the side. Don't forget to fill the wineglasses to the brim. And, in my case, say proudly, "Esterhazy Kupecsirke!"

Take-a-Nap
Chicken and Rice

· ·

- **chicken**
- **1 onion**
- **salt, pepper, paprika**
- **butter, margarine or oil**
- **rice**
- **bouillon cube**

(The glory of this recipe is that you can fiddle around with the chicken and the rice quantities according to how many you are serving. The measurement police aren't going to come after you, as long the proportion of rice to chicken is to your liking.)

In a big heavy pot, brown onion, salt, pepper, and paprika in butter, margarine, or oil. I don't care what your preference is, just do it. Throw in the chicken and brown that too, turning and smacking it around so it knows who is boss. (Alternatively, if you are a spiritual sort of cook, pick it up preciously and murmur little sweet nothings to it. But then that means you will begin to bond with the chicken. Good luck eating it.)

In a separate pot, cook up a few

cups of rice with the correct amount of water. (One cup rice, two cups water, etc.) Throw in a bouillon cube and don't think about the additives. You are a desperate Rebel Cook and you don't have time to worry about such things.

Once the rice and water are boiling, pour it into the pot with the chicken, stir it, turn down the heat to just above simmering, and put the lid on it. Fall into a comfy chair with a glass of something and a nice magazine. Put your feet up, take a snooze for an hour or so. Then get up, lift the lid, make sure nothing has burned, and add some more salt, pepper, and paprika if you feel like it. If your guests are expected soon, you may wish to run around the house with a vacuum cleaner and Swiffer, flinging dishes on the table and preparing to be a gracious hostess.

Give me marks for courage. I am a Rebel Cook. No matter how many times I am knocked to the floor in failure and humiliation, I rise again and try to put something on the table that is edible. Or, even better, try to fool people into thinking it might be edible, or not even noticing whether or not it is edible.

WHEN THE WOLF IS AT THE DOOR
(WITH HOMAGE TO M. F. K. FISHER)

Some of you may operate under the assumption that entertaining is expensive. Well, yes, it is, if you are going to hire a string quartet, a band of gypsy musicians, or the Cirque du Soleil troupe, serve $25 bottles of wine and chateaubriand, or maybe fly in a nice arctic char by private jet.

That would be delightful, but one can have just as much fun in steerage, without pots of money, as long as one does it with panache.

I have entertained at times when common sense told me I should instead save my money for the electricity bill. Alas, sometimes unhappy circumstances can smash into each other, and one is suddenly contemplating a dinner to which one has invited a host of people without adequate funds. Fear not.

In a pinch, you can do dinner for six on less than $20. It won't be a great dinner, but it will do. (As long as at least three people bring wine.) Just because you don't have any money, don't be intimidated into feeling deprived, impoverished, or desperate. You must rise above your circumstances with the precious commodity that money can't buy: style.

One of the most fabulous dinners I ever ate was at the home of a friend on a limited income. I had suffered through dental surgery earlier in the day and was feeling rather limp when I arrived at her home. She was a magnificent cook who followed the vegetarian path and shopped frugally but carefully. First, she served a lentil soup laden with garlic. Then, a small salad laced with garlic dressing. Then, a whole wheat pasta with mushrooms and peppers, permeated with garlic. I may have smelled like a kielbasa when I left her place, but, yow, I was healthy and I was happy and I was chock-full of garlic, one of the best possible things for your health and heart.

"She put them together with thought and gratitude, and never seemed to realize that her cuisine was one of intense romantic strangeness to everyone but herself. I doubt if she spent more than fifty dollars a year on what she and her entranced guests ate, but from the gracious abstracted way she gave you a soup dish full of sliced cactus leaves and lemonberries and dried crumbled kelp, it might as well have been stuffed ortolans."

M. F. K. Fisher, *How to Cook a Wolf*

If you are entertaining on the cheap, you can do it cheap cheep surprisingly easily. Get your chicken on sale. The little cluckers don't care if they are bargain biddies. Go the inexpensive route and put in the extra effort to jazz it up. True, none of this will make people leap out of their chairs, shouting "Oh my God, what an extravagant dinner! You shouldn't have spent so much!" but if the meal is prepared prudently, or at least with a minimum of hysteria, you might be able to get away with it.

Inexpensive wine (and generous guests), staples bought on sale, simple food artfully presented, and an environment made appealing by your own personality can add up to a magical evening. The trick is balancing your own shortcomings (be they financial or culinary) with your fervent desire to please your guests. Sincere warmth and kindness is great currency, much more valuable than the actual coin in hand, and can make even the most modest gathering extravagant.

the ohmygodihaveinvitedpeopleto-dinnerandthedarnedchequedidn't-arriveandwhatamigoingtodoand-whenisthenexttraintoinuvik dinner

The stock market crashed, your company suddenly folded and you're out of a job, the furnace went on the blink and you had to use every available penny to keep from freezing to death, your bank doesn't remember who you are, and you still have eight people coming for dinner that very evening, expecting food. Before you hurl yourself from your roof onto the top of the nearest passing garbage truck to make your getaway, examine your resources for a bare bones meal.

Appetizers

Crackers (even if you found them at the back of your cupboard and they date back to Queen Elizabeth's coronation) and a hunk of cheese, any cheese. Plus anything you can find in your refrigerator that has some colour that you can slice into pretty or eccentric shapes. Even a pathetic tomato or a lonely little apple will do. Put it on a pretty platter as if it were a gourmet treat and don't apologize.

continued...

Wine

There are some great California wines for $7 or $8 a bottle, plus you can usually count on most guests bringing a bottle. If any of your very dearest and closest and most adorable friends are coming, you can phone in desperation and ask them to bring a bottle. On the rare occasions I have done this, the dear darling delightful angels have shown up with three bottles.

Ginger garlic chicken

Chicken thighs marinated in garlic cloves and ginger and olive oil (or a ginger sauce if you have a bottle hanging around) ... chicken thighs bought on sale, natch.

Rice

Cheap, cheap, cheap, and you can dress it up with onions or mushrooms or whatever is hanging around that isn't black and mouldy, which you can throw into the frying pan and sauté like crazy, then add to the cooking rice (one cup rice, two cups water, put the lid on, turn down the heat, and say a prayer of thanks for rice, the easiest and cheapest thing in the world to make).

Vegetable

Forage in the refrigerator, and whatever you pull out — whether it is turnip, parsnip, zucchini, or a wrinkled old green pepper — wash it, slice it, throw it in the microwave, add

a few raisins, butter, and curry powder. Most people (if they have drunk enough) will swear it is an exotic recipe. Fallback: close your eyes and open a can of corn or peas and add something that will jazz it up. Final stand: find that old bottle of caraway liqueur/rye/gin in the back of the cupboard and pour it on. After two bites, they won't even know what they are eating.

Salad

Who says a salad has to be romaine or iceberg? If you have an apple, a few sticks of celery, and some nuts or raisins, mix them up and pile fetchingly on pretty plates as if you have mastered nouvelle cuisine. Make sure you use an enormous plate. The very best restaurants know they can fool people into thinking they are getting something incredibly rare and special if it is served on a plate the size of a truck tire with a tiny little blob of food in Othe middle.

Dessert

Ask somebody to bring it. In my experience, most guests offer to bring dessert in self-defence. At one dinner, I had six desserts, just because they had all tasted my attempts at baking on other occasions.

If presented with care, all will be well. Nobody comes to my joint for the food, anyway.

set decoration: costumes, props, and invisible guests

> *"The hostess must be like the duck – calm and unruffled*
> *on the surface, and paddling like hell underneath."*
>
> PLOTS AND PANS

*B*efore your guests so much as choke on a stale cracker in your home, their senses will be enlivened, touched, or attacked by their first impressions. They will form an opinion of what lies ahead upon viewing your home. (A goat tethered to the front railing is never a good sign.) They may nod in approval, sigh happily, or shudder when they first lay eyes upon the little hostess. (It is advisable to be attired. For instance, don't do the naked-in-foil thing recommended by pop magazines in the '70s. This could lead to certain conclusions about your intentions.) They will also guess at what the future holds if the music you are playing full blast is vintage Def Leppard. They are innocents, putting the next few hours of their lives in your hands. Be kind. The first sight of you and your abode should be reassuring, not discouraging or frightening.

WHAT TO WEAR …

We all have different notions of appropriate garb for dinner. I once had hosts insist that I come to dinner wearing blue jeans, because, they said, they wanted me to be "comfortable." Little did they know that I had but one pair of ancient and decidedly unstylish jeans, which I found excruciatingly uncomfortable, rather like wearing two dark blue washboards, and in which I felt like one of the Beverly Hillbillies. I wore the jeans to please the hosts (postmodern hippies) and was miserable.

So if your guests ask you "What shall I wear?" respond with accuracy and flexibility. It is perfectly reasonable to want to know the parameters of the dress for the event. When people ask, it means they want to be comfortable in the context of the evening.

Sometimes the host can give you a definite wrong turn. I was once told by a hostess to wear my "party clothes" and so I did. I showed up in a floor-length velvet dress with 10 pounds of jewellery and big hair. Everybody else was wearing faded denim or sweats. (Luckily, there was a transsexual in the assembly, and those who were not accustomed to hearing a baritone coming out of the mouth of a gorgeous blond were so riveted by the experience that nobody noticed me or what I was wearing.)

A few little hints are just fine, like "Don't wear the suit of armour you wore to the medieval re-enactment last autumn." Let them know that they are free to dress comfortably, but, just in case they are nudists and take this too literally, you could add "To my home, some men come in sports jackets, some wear sweaters, and some women wear long skirts, but others wear casual slacks." Something vague and reassuring that will give some guidelines but not be oppressively directive, like "Wear taffeta, we want you to be comfortable" or "Wear jeans, we want you to be *comfortable*."

As the host or hostess, you have an obligation to set the tone of the evening. Choose your wardrobe so that it is neither fancy enough to embarrass the guest who arrives in cords, nor so slovenly that the guest in a suit is mortified. I aspire to an Anaïs Nin sort of hospitality: velvet, embroidery, or tapestry. This is a win-win situation as the gypsy/ethnic artist look can be either dressy or casual and transcends all categorizations. Unfortunately, this may be hard to carry off if you are a) 16 months' pregnant b) the fullback on your football team or c) a Mafia hitman. Not that I want to discourage anybody from sartorial self-expression.

A major doyenne of the domestic arts has been berated in the press for accepting an invitation as guest speaker at a black tie charity event, then showing up fresh (or not so fresh) from a hike in the mountains, wearing her hiking garb, hair windblown, and personality more suited to interaction with grizzly bears than the starstruck guests, who had shelled out several thousand dollars for the thrill of being in the same room with her.

We all need to respect the occasion and the efforts that both host and guests have invested in it. Guests at one of my dinners were somewhat taken aback when two latecomers straggled in after a long day of golfing, obviously not having bothered with a comb or toothbrush after a fine old day out on the greens with the dust, the sun, the grass, and the insects. The rest of us were not in black tie, but most of us had at least taken a bath at some point in the day. Nobody shuffled their chairs away from the two golfers, but it was a reminder that none of us like to dine with people with dead caterpillars in their hair.

On the other hand, most of us feel a little awkward when we are overdressed for an event. Women often do that, inspired by media, fashion magazines, and Manolo Blahnik. I am also motivated by the fact that I spend 80 percent of my time in flannel jammies with sheep or teddy bears on them, bunny slippers on my feet, and my hair sticking up in 15 directions like Woody Woodpecker, glued to the computer, trying to construct meaningful and lucrative sentences. Therefore, any opportunity to dress like a grown-up is an exciting event, and I usually try on 25 outfits (which I may not have worn in five years) before I find one that a) fits me and b) is not ridiculously out of date.

... OR NOT

- Lingerie. You want to distract people from your cooking but not to the point where they either stare at you relentlessly in stunned horror or glance desperately around the room, trying not to look at you. (I have accidentally done this, due to a certain misreading of a page in a fashion magazine, and the evening was Not Fun.)

- Anything highly flammable. Not until you have a very strong and secure relationship with oil and your stove should you wear any of that weird polyester that ignites in a second.

- Large pink Velcro rollers. This does not set the stage for an elegant evening. Also, very few people, male or female, look good wearing them.

- Anything bulky or Elizabethan in nature, unless you live in a castle. Otherwise, you will be squeezing

around a table trying to
serve people without be-
heading them.

- Nothing so weird that halfway
  through the evening, you suddenly look in a mirror, gasp, say
  to yourself "What was I thinking?"
  and then faint dead away. This will slow
  down dinner big time.

If a guest arrives in a costume that is totally out of place, do not make them feel even more
dreadful by commenting on it. I know this seems obvious, but oh the woes of the unbelievable words that
come out of our mouth and hang in a balloon over our
head at the most inopportune times! So do not say to
friend Faron, "My goodness, are you overdressed or
what!" Nor do you say to your friend the caterpillar-
laden golfer, "Oh yucch, are there no showers at the
golf course?" You can squawk about it later to yourself
in the confines of your bathroom, where many an ani-
mated conversation may take place about such topics,
but, as the Rebel Cook and hostess, you will be resolutely polite.

We have all made horrible mistakes in wardrobe
and must forgive ourselves. I have almost (but not
quite) erased the memory of attending a party some

ode to the apron

In my Home Economics class decades ago, each student was required to report to the teacher with progress on the apron we were sewing. The teacher (whose name I mercifully forget) stared at the ragged, clumsily basted piece of huck cloth I held in my hands for a long moment, then slowly lowered her head to her desk. Her shoulders heaved, and I heard a few little gasps. I believe she was crying. Or laughing.

The only reason my apron was eventually sewn and completed, a requirement for passing the course, was because five of my classmates — appalled at the thought that I, the dear little egghead with the thick glasses, might fail — took turns surreptitiously sewing my apron for me. I am now excessively fond of aprons, perhaps because they represent kindness and caring to me.

Aprons are wonderful, fussy, practical inventions. Sadly, they're rarely worn anymore, unless they sport ghastly politically incorrect sayings. Somebody once gave me an apron with "Bitch Bitch Bitch" printed on it in giant letters. I didn't quite know how to take it, but at the time it was my only apron and I got into the habit of wearing it. After a while, I forgot what it said and perhaps shocked a few dozen guests over the years with my cheerful obliviousness. Now I have a lovely selection of vintage aprons that are great fun to wear. And in much better taste.

The apron has several uses. The most important is the protection of your clothes while you are cooking. A grease spatter on an apron is negligible. On a Ralph Lauren shirt, it is cause for tears. And I shed enough of those in the mere act of making a salad.

An apron can also make a statement. If it is vintage, it can remind people of their childhood. There is something about wearing a sweet, old-fashioned apron that is endearing, perhaps because it sends the message that we aren't too serious about our dignity. A woman wearing an apron is comforting. A man good-humoured enough to don one and greet guests at the door is downright delightful. As an added bonus, wearing an apron fools guests into thinking you are actually cooking something.

20 years ago in which I inexplicably attired myself in a pantsuit made from a bright green sari, a pantsuit of thin silk that clung to me extremely inappropriately and was as alien to the extremely conservative nature of the other guests as I was to the notion of appearing anywhere in public semi-clothed. It is always a good idea to remember the public humiliations of our past: it keeps us humble and not too inclined to crab at other people.

Ultimately, what we wear to dinner is not nearly as important as what we say and what we do. You could wear a ratty potato sack, but as long as you are kind, polite, considerate, and charming (and bring a bottle or two), all will be forgiven.

The First Sighting: Guests on the Horizon

Ahoy! From a distance you spy the guests sailing your way. They, in turn, are looking for a building that matches your address.

I will be so bold as to make some obvious suggestions: The first thing to consider is the view of your humble home from the exterior. Is the front porch light on? Is the address clearly visible? (If these questions are revelations to you, perhaps this explains why some of your dinners have been delayed by an hour or so, as would-be guests drive around and around the neighbourhood looking for the party.) And by the way, if you live on a crescent, or in a neighbourhood where all the streets intersect and mate and mutate in strange and mysterious ways, directions wouldn't hurt either. Sending an e-mail to all with specific directions from every part of the city shows that you really are interested in their safe arrival at your door. (I once requested directions to a party and was asked impatiently by the host, "Don't you have a map?" He is otherwise a perfect gentleman. He just must have a thing about giving directions.)

If you live in a wintry clime (and who in this country doesn't?), consider the snow. Alas, once it lands, somebody has to shovel it. If you are not wealthy enough to hire a snow removal service, are not masochistic enough to have a teenager in your possession, and have not been fortunate enough to blackmail the neighbours (with their uncurtained windows) into shovelling it for you, the task is yours. No guest will feel welcome or jolly after struggling through a foot of snow to reach your door.

Even worse is ice. I was once invited to a rather lavish New Year's house party in Toronto. Unbelievably, the front walk, steepled with high steps, was an ice sculpture of cubism. Every step was like a vertical slide into the air, then down, and a wild slide onto the next foot. We looked like demented ice skaters by the time we made it to the door. To this day, I do not know how my companion and I did not end up sprawled like pretzels in the snow. And I wonder about the hosts. If they knew they had invited approximately 30 people to dinner and drink (and I assume they did, unless they were hopeless drunks and had extended the invitations during a binge), why did they not at least put a pinch of sand or salt on their Everest-like steps? Were they secret murderers, hoping that at least half the guests would meet a violent demise before the party? (Perhaps that explains the paucity of dinner that evening, and the preponderance of generic potato chips.)

It is also useful to have a doorbell that works. And, with any luck, that doorbell will ring. Then, you, the little host or hostess, open the door.

This is very important. No matter what has just exploded in the microwave or oven, no matter what has just overflowed, smoked, burned, crumbled, imploded, or hurt you grievously, you must have a smile on your face. These are your guests, and this is your mantra: you have invited people to your house because you like them (we hope) and because you want to make them feel welcome and valued. Not everybody (however intelligent and educated) has quite caught on to this (what seems to me) obvious tenet.

For example, I have been invited to dinner at homes where, upon ringing the doorbell, I have been greeted by the teenage offspring of the host, who has promptly walked away after opening the door. The host was nowhere to be seen. So I, the guest, was left to fumble around, looking for a closet in which to hang my coat (which nobody offered to take from me) and amble around looking for the kitchen with my bottle of wine (for which nobody thanked me). Lovely as these people were, I didn't feel particularly valued.

> *"One must always welcome guests sincerely, with a certain effusion of the heart, for when they come to your table they must already be happy with you."*
>
> BARON LÉON BRISSE, *LA PETITE CUISINE DU BARON BRISSE* (1870)

Recently, I arrived at the home of highly educated friends (not that education guarantees sophistication, but those of us who have a few degrees cling to this hope) and upon ringing the doorbell was indeed greeted by the host. Who disappeared. I entered in the hope that in fact my presence was welcome and was somewhat bemused to discover host and hostess engaged in conversation unrelated to myself in the kitchen. What to do? Was my presence desired? Or not? Or was I, in the style of the free-for-all '60s and '70s, supposed to stomp my way through the house, light up a joint, and collapse into a chair, scratching my stomach and grunting "So, got any food, man?"

I vaguely recall substance-soaked bashes from university days that had that sort of informality, a milieu in which manners were considered artificial and an impediment to communication, and in which locks were taken off bathroom doors to further facilitate happy sharing. Nobody was ever introduced or welcomed because it was just toooo superficial. Personally, I prefer parties where the host takes you by your little hand and leads you around the room and introduces you to one and all as if you are a Really Important Person.

This is my longwinded way of saying that, no matter what your state, your demeanour, your angst, your allergies, your level of inebriation — when the doorbell rings, and the people on the other side of the door are the very ones that you, in your silliness, have invited to dinner, and they have arrived at the appropriate hour, you must fling yourself upon them and greet them as if they were the very most important people in your life.

For, in fact, at that moment, they are. They are your guests. And you have invited them. And therefore you have made the commitment to make them feel honoured and special. No excuses. No matter what they do. (Unless: they set the house on fire, then press charges. If they bring pets or children uninvited, narrow your eyes, and cross them off your list.)

Dazzle Them with Décor
(Then Confound Them with Clutter)

The guests stand before you, their faces lit with expectation. No turning back now. You and they are both trapped. They anticipate dinner. You can hold them off for a while if you overwhelm them with style (or, in my case, plain old clutter).

Lady Mendl, in 1930s Paris, was renowned for the lavish and imaginative décor at her soirées. Apparently, the food was often dreadful, but it is the memory of her décor that prevails in history. So duping them with décor isn't anything new. You just have to find new ways to do it.

I am not advocating that you redecorate your home in harem style or bring in a pride of lions to liven things up. Nor am I advising that you hire an interior designer. If you are going to do that, for goodness' sake, just skip to the end of the book and hire a caterer. End of problem. (End of book. Stop reading now and get out there and celebrate.)

However, a well-appointed home, with just enough knick-knacks and obscure items hanging about to catch a person's attention, is a definite ally in your battle. A photo of you with a famous astronaut, a prime minister, or a rock star discreetly placed at eye level as they enter the room can be very handy. If you are desperate, a nude or compromising photo of yourself will do the trick.

The whole notion of hospitality is that you want people to feel relaxed and comfortable. I have been in moneyed estates where the tiled floors were so cold that one wanted a hot water bottle from the butler just to get through the dinner. I have been invited to dinner on a cool autumn night and have been seated, inexplicably, in front of the open patio door, with icy winds blowing my hair and salad into disarray. (I finally wrapped my feet in the tablecloth.) And then I have been in tiny rooms where the music, the food, and the company were so wonderful that I didn't care whether the rugs had been vacuumed or the food was epicurean.

Yes, entertaining is a heck of a lot of work, and I for one am reduced at some point, usually just before the guests arrive, to wailing and weeping in the kitchen and wishing I could climb into the breadbox and not come out until dinner was over.

However, if you are an enterprising person with any sort of a life beyond the kitchen, you will be saved by your décor. In my living room, every piece of art and furniture has a story — relating to sentiment, anecdote, folly, or history — that can be used to fuel conversation. So if there are deadly silences, I can easily point guests to some decaying artifact or dust-laden knick-knack, tell them its provenance, and usually, with luck, this starts a conversation. Then I am free to disappear into the kitchen and fight with the chicken and negotiate with the vegetables.

If you are a collector, you are forearmed. Your home is no doubt packed with memorabilia and antiques that will provoke comment. People tell me they love coming to my place because it is "festive" and "full of stories." This happened by accident. You can do the same on purpose, if it makes entertaining easier, and you might actually have fun doing it.

"It is an omen of success for her evening if the hostess can make conversation general before dinner. To this end, have some novelty at hand, either in the shape of a personage whom everybody wants to meet, or a new picture, a grotesque group, a rare plant in the drawing-room, the latest spice of news to tell, or a pretty girl to bring forward. Whatever the attraction, bring it on at once, to prevent that very stupid half hour."

THE HOME COOK BOOK (1887)

If you have, sadly, bought every piece of furniture and art in your living room from a generic warehouse store, do not despair. At least one of your guests (we hope, tactfully) will seek to inform you on how to improve. This will at least get a few sentences zinging back and forth.

A home with personality will invite comment. An

awkward pause can be bridged by a casual comment on the garlic sausage wreath hanging from the mantel or the black velvet painting of the Last Supper covering an entire wall. (Although some people might take this way too literally.) Unusual ornaments inspire conversation. (As in, "Don't you love this gigantic stuffed teddy bear? However did she fit it through her door? Oh, whoops, don't fall over that — oh dear, does anybody have a splint? Can you breathe? Can you get your nose out of the bear's ear? Does anybody know CPR?")

Next: the walls. Do not repaint the interior of your house in anticipation of a dinner party. I am all for as little work as possible. In fact, I am all for falling onto the sofa with a box of chocolates and a nice goblet of Benedictine.

> "No matter how talented a woman may be, or how useful in the church or society, if she is an indifferent housekeeper it is fatal to her influence, a foil to her brilliancy and a blemish in her garments."
>
> THE HOME COOK BOOK (1887)

However, may I ask what colour your walls are? Oh, please don't fall about, cursing at me as one of those "what colour are you?" pundits. Just let me make a few points: One of the very worst parties I ever attended (ever) was in an upscale house where the walls were painted black and (I kid you not) the host had asked everybody to dress in white. He wore black. It was damned weird and unsettling, and not my idea of a good time. I have a vague memory of being chased around the black and white furnace in the black and white basement.

The most wonderful dinner parties I hosted were in a tiny bungalow in which the walls had been painted peach, a warming and restful colour. Again and again, people told me that when they entered that room, they felt safe and peaceful. The colours with which you greet your guests will help create the mood you wish. Peach, pink, and blue are restful and relaxing. Linda Clark's book *The Ancient Art of Color Therapy* is a wonderful reference for colour coding your home. Whether you follow her advice totally or partially, it will help you choose your colours well.

OF CATS AND DOGS
AND VACUUM CLEANERS AND RESPIRATORS

I am, of course, assuming, that your home is clean, and that your guests' feet will not be trailing dust bunnies as they engage in existential or glamorous gossip. Have you done your cleaning?

This again is a dilemma. Like many obsessive compulsives, I feel that every corner of my home, including under the kitchen sink (which all guests automatically check when they are looking for their coats, right?), under my bed (which every single guest will check while looking for the washroom, right?), and the back porch landing (which every guest will check out while heading to their car, which is in front of the house, right?), must be scrupulously clean before a dinner party.

I am the worst person to give advice on this subject. I am the most horrible example of the person who cleans all the wrong things, all the stupidest, unreachable areas, just because somebody might open a cupboard and uncover my secret horror: I am not a perfect housekeeper.

Is this how I (or anybody) should be spending my time? We must make the assumption that anybody we choose to invite to our house is of sufficient substance that they are far beyond counting dust bunnies.

Personally, I would rather experience dust bunnies than cats. There are an amazing number of people who have no idea that the first smell that greets a visitor on the opening of their door is Cat You-Know-What. Gee, how wonderful. Really makes you feel like relaxing into a lovely meal ... Especially when you sink into the sofa and cat hairs rise around you like an aura. And when you sit down to dinner and the cat hairs are clinging to your wineglass and plate.

I have been in homes where cats crawled evilly around one's lap while the hostess smiled benignly; I have been in homes where cats snarled and attacked, with the host's bland eye nodding in approval; I once attended an exquisite tea in an elegant home so permeated with cat that my eyes clouded over and I could not see to drive home.

Cat lovers are not about to send their cats overseas. However, they might consider the benefits of Febreeze or some nice natural candle scents. A thorough vacuuming of carpets and cats is also highly recommended. Fumigation wouldn't hurt either, in my opinion, but then, I am violently allergic to cats and may be prejudiced.

Having said that, I prefer cats to killer dogs. Friends were once trapped in a home with a mastiff that lunged and snapped at their every move while the elderly hostess watched, smiling all the while. The dog ate my friend's earring. The next bite nearly turned her husband into her wife. When they finally escaped to their car, they fell into each other's arms and trembled for half an hour. Now, I ask you, what sort of dinner party was that?

"The ultimate aim of civility and good manners is to please: to please one's guest or to please one's host. To this end one uses the rules laid down by tradition: of welcome, generosity, affability, cheerfulness and consideration for others."

CLAUDIA RODEN, *A BOOK OF MIDDLE EASTERN FOOD*

SOFT SEATS AND SAFE COFFEE TABLES

As somebody who has made myriad mistakes in seating arrangements (including the time I sat a guest on a chair that fell apart and, even worse, the time I sat on a guest) I have a lot of nerve giving advice. At least I have never made grown-up persons sit on pillows on

yoohoo! where are you? are you there?

Lighting — it is always useful to have some.

Too much is obnoxious and gives people migraines. Too little leads to misunderstandings, like Ms. X fondling Mr. B when she really meant to get chummy with Mr. T. Too little can also lead to people eating candles, ornately folded napkins, and butter knives they have mistaken for food.

Do you have every light in the house blazing, so that those with incipient migraines immediately shade their eyes or pull their sweater over their head? This may be a hint that your lights are too bright. On the other hand, if you create an atmosphere that is somewhat reminiscent of the ambience of *Alien*, various of your guests may wander into the living room, trip on your folk art display, and end up cold as a mackerel in your lovely artificial fish pond.

My advice is to err on the side of under-lighting, for purely practical reasons. The less people can see, the less you have to dust. I would prefer to have a few kerosene lamps in the corners and guide people to their chairs if it meant less work in the dusting department.

It is also a good idea not to have floor lamps that attack

people. I have this bad habit of acquiring vintage floor lamps with wonderfully ornate features that, unfortunately, like a swamp creature want to cling and trip and bonk guests on the head. So move these things to another room during a dinner party unless you have murder on your mind.

However, the most wonderful piece of advice I ever received in the lighting department was the following: Pink.

Pink light bulbs are available at most department stores, and once you install them, there is no turning back. The pink light creates a warm atmosphere that is undeniably comforting. When people tell me they feel relaxed and serene in my home, I nod and smile, giv-

ing the impression that I know it is because of my extraordinary aura. But, in my heart of hearts, I know it is the pink light bulbs.

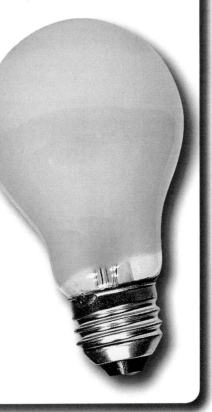

the floor, which thank goodness is a sin to which I have never sunk.

First, check the room to make sure you have a comfortable perch for every guest. Even though your sofa may look absolutely wonderful with 35 stuffed toys adorning it, in deference to your guests, you should probably take a few dozen of said animals away. It's a life decision: the toys or the guests.

For a while, I kept cute stuffed bears and rabbits on the back of the sofa, until finally I went beyond mildly noting that some fell on the heads of the guests and actually noticed that one guest heaved one across the room after it fell on his head for the fifth time. This was a wakeup call. Yes, I want a cute and lovable home. But I also want my guests to feel comfortable. And to make intelligent conversation as opposed to brutalizing my stuffed animals.

Although I do not want to dictate what should be on a coffee table (snacks would be nice), I can definitely tell you what should *not* be on a coffee table: intimate portraits taken of any member of the family with either human or animal, toenail clippings (the only reason I include this is because I have in fact been invited to a home where the only item on the coffee table was toenail clippings — and you thought YOU led a sheltered life), and a bowl full of marbles. Although this last tip may apply to only a small segment of the population (i.e., marble collectors like me), after you have seen an unsuspecting guest pick up a marble and put it in his mouth, thinking it is a candy that cleverly resembles a marble, and then dealt with the ensuing medical crisis, you will forever banish bowls of marbles from your coffee table. (Unless you enjoy lawsuits.)

BEWARE BOYFRIENDS, BUBBLES, AND BOORS

Despite all your plotting and planning, things can go awry, no matter what you do. At times, your home may be "redecorated" through unfortunate circumstances: natural disasters, drunkenness, and the wild card guest.

I once invited an old friend, her boyfriend, her mother, and my mother to Christmas dinner. What was I thinking?

My mother was my only ally in a meal doomed to failure. The evening was punctuated by menacing, sepulchral, slowly paced pronouncements from The Boyfriend, who appeared to be battling either a drug problem or a temptation to become a serial killer. The two mothers retreated into fantasyland, pretending everything was normal. I went into the kitchen and started praying. My friend came into the kitchen and was perfectly cheery and lovely, except for the fact that the wineglass in her hand shattered as she held it.

The evening skidded downhill relentlessly. My old friend (having managed to acquire more wine) hauled the Brussels sprouts out of the microwave in order to fling her plum pudding into the recesses of the poor appliance. We not only ate half-frozen Brussels sprouts, but she attacked the plum pudding with such viciousness that my kitchen floor was carpeted with brown gunk that took days to remove. (I suppose that cynics will think I am exaggerating. I have no way to prove it, but my memory is vivid: my brilliant white linoleum was covered with hunks and piles of dark brown pudding. It stuck to my slippers. It smeared. It smelled. The linoleum was barely visible, and it never recovered. I finally sold the house so that I could escape that floor.)

The lessons in this are the following:

1. Keep possession of your microwave at all times — allow no one to appropriate it.

2. Be careful who you invite to Christmas dinner.

Another little glitch is the guest who inadvertently damages the house. This is why we have insurance companies. The good little guest who accidentally tips over the Tiffany lamp will whip out a notebook and pen and dash off the name of their insurance company before trotting out the door to lie down in the middle of the road, hoping a truck will put them out of their misery.

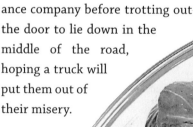

I have a friend who, when invited to a soirée so that the hosts could show off their new snow-white shag rug, was asked to open the red wine as the hosts greeted other guests. He opened the red wine all over the new rug and spent the next five minutes moving every piece of furniture he could in order to cover the damage.

Not all of us have that option. Recently, I dined at a table set with the hostess's most precious possession, her Royal Crown Derby Blue Mikado china. I was wearing a recent addition to my vintage jewellery collection, a lovely glass pendant. As I pulled my chair to the table, my heavy glass pendant swung right into the nearest plate with a clang that created a breathless pause that hung in the air for a good minute.

I spent the rest of the dinner constantly rubbing the edge of the plate to reassure myself and everybody else that there was no chip. "No chip!" I would chirp brightly, every five minutes. "See! No chip!" It later occurred to me that I probably rubbed off some of the trim with that nervous reassurance. But at least there was No Chip!

I lay awake that night thinking of the Peter Sellers' film *The Party*, in which Sellers' character sets in motion a chain of events that results in the house being drowned in giant bubbles and a baby elephant parading through. I had to reassure myself that I was Not That Bad — the house was still standing and there was at least no elephant in the room.

Bubbles at least are innocuous. What about germs — pandemic or garden variety? For the guest who shows up at your door doubled over in a coughing fit and gasping "It's the bubonic plague, but I didn't want to miss your party," it is handy to have a little table and chair, with a candle, set up in the broom closet. Even though you may want to boot them out the door, you, as the adorable host or hostess, are required to admit them. Just settle them and their germs into that broom closet and they won't be coming back any time soon when they have the plague. You don't want them killing off the other guests before the meal has a chance to do the job. I once attended a huge party where one of the best-known stuntmen in the west was so toxic with flu that half the guests (myself included) spent the next three weeks hacking and wheezing in bed. We're talking nearly 300 people.

Some come bearing a thing far worse than germs: bad manners. I have had guests examine my drapes critically and proclaim, dramatically, "Those are bad. This is terrible. You need to have these hung properly." I know of a woman whose guest picked up every cushion on her sofa and shook it for dust. I have seen people run their fingers along the piano checking for dust trails. I have heard of people trouncing into homes and belittling the carpets ("These are threadbare") or the kitchen chairs ("These are falling apart").

Excuse me if I sound a little tough here — but these are people that one doesn't need trampling one's spirit. I am fragile enough in the kitchen. To have somebody disturb my already uncertain equilibrium is asking for trouble. I am appalled by what horrific behaviour people seem to think is acceptable. If one accepts it.

Luckily, of course, you don't have to. You can choose your guests — and the guests you choose are more interested in the conversation, the other guests, the music, and the aesthetic of the evening than how much you paid for your carpets. It is more usual for my guests to tour my collections, exclaiming over my ceramics, glass, Victorian prints, buttons, and eclectic arrangements of kitsch and elegance.

The solution: Don't invite clods and boors to your home. But sometimes you don't know they are clods and boors until they are inside the doors, and what do you do then? Discreetly pick up the phone and dial the number of the local etiquette police? As the gracious host or hostess, you smile serenely, knowing bad karma will strike these people, most ideally with a battalion of mice in their kitchen shelves. (Not that mice are a bad thing.)

Of Course You Set the Table Yesterday ... Didn't You?

The first sighting of a beautifully set table can transport and deceive a guest into believing that an extraordinary meal will appear. As a Rebel Cook, you should do everything possible to encourage this mad and sweet dream. I have served extraordinary meals, but they were extraordinary for reasons other than epicurean.

Let us assume that you have a decent-sized dining table, suitable for eight people. If this is the case, congratulations. You can set up a dinner with china and silverware without undue fuss. But, to be realistic, not all of us have that luxury or live in mansions, or even reasonably large homes. There are brilliant simple tricks — fallback positions — to manufacturing elegance out of nothing. All it takes is opening your mind to the possibilities.

Suppose you live in a dreary little one-room apartment and desperately want to give a dinner party. But with no room for a table for two, to say nothing of a table for eight, your options appear to be the floor or the kitchen counter. Remember, improvisation is a gift. Do you have a trunk and a tablecloth? Do you have packing crates and a bedspread? In fact, as long as you have a reasonably appealing (and clean — this is important!) piece of material, you can work wonders with boxes, trunks, and weird objects. Your guests will be delighted by your inventiveness and the care you took to make the evening special for them.

(Perhaps I seem to harp on clean. Am I the only person in the world who remembers the odious days of '70s hospitality, when hosts threw all sorts of grunge on the table and then snarled at you, "It's all organic"? It seems to me that, although one shouldn't be obsessively germophobic, it makes sense to present a relatively clean table, perhaps free of dust clumps, mould, or fungus. Then, perhaps I am being picky.)

Often, we have to depend on the art of illusion to create elegance in our dinner parties. One of my friends, a brilliant but underemployed performer, transformed her closet-sized dining room with mirrored walls, giving fabulous dinner parties in the illusion of space, openness, and affluence.

It is also handy to seat yourself at every chair at the table and take note of what you see. Will one person stare straight into a pile of old newspapers spewing out of a ratty canvas bag? You may not have noticed it when you cleaned the hallway, but there it is, like a nasty fungus, destroying your careful arrangement in the living room.

"Although (the hostess) may spend many hours thus employed and will be under the impression the room is as elegant as she can make it, five minutes after the first guest has arrived she will perceive that in the very centre of the mantelpiece there rests a thermometer, a bottle of ink, two orange sticks and an india rubber ..."

Virginia Graham, *Say Please* (1949)

At one of my most vibrant parties, I looked around the kitchen as people chatted before dinner, thinking that things were going splendidly (and indeed they were). "Yes," I breathed to myself, "I am finally a perfect hostess. People are talking, laughing, drinking. The music is great. The appetizers didn't send anybody screaming from the house, crying for Maalox. The house is clean and appealing ..."

That is when I looked at the top of the fridge and saw It. The horrible, rusted, scarred, filthy metal roaster that I had briefly considered — for about two and a half seconds — as a possible container for the chicken, and that I had discarded as being too revolting — and that I was sure I had taken downstairs en route to the Dumpster.

But no! It was there, on top of the fridge, halfway out of a plastic grocery bag — sitting there, gloriously obnoxious and distasteful. I remembered that I had put it aside by the door to the basement, then forgotten about it. Some guest, trying to be helpful, had decided to move it where it was not underfoot, to the top of the fridge, where everybody could see it. A great cook would not be bothered by this. But a desperate Rebel Cook still cringes at the memory, as the party depended, not on her food, but on the company and the atmosphere — and the décor.

Ultimately, you want your guests, when they enter, to feel comfortable, welcome, and at peace. At the very least, lock your Doberman in the garage, try for half a chair per guest, and pick up any nails or thumbtacks you may have left on the floor.

DÉCOR ON A DIME

Whenever I falter on entertaining because I do not possess the latest, the most expensive, footstools or corkscrews in existence, I remind myself of the great artists who entertained with elegance in impoverished circumstances. I may not have the cachet of living in Paris in the 1920s, but I do what I can on the Canadian prairie. If one has a creative soul, one can find ways to make magic with found items. And even if you think you do not have a creative soul, simply embarking on the search for treasures may spark inventiveness and imagination you did not think you had.

Some of the most delightful homes I have set foot in have been homes furnished from recycled treasures. I know an artist who has layered her home

"The usual should be made unusual; extraordinariness should cloak the ordinary."

M. F. K. FISHER,
AN ALPHABET FOR GOURMETS

with a combination of antiques, souvenir items, and toys. The cost in money was minimal. The time and energy was something else, but to her, it was a joy and an entrancement.

Furnish your home and set your table with things you love, and it will show. You don't need to reveal that you cleaned out a few rummage sales to get the stuff unless you choose to. I am shameless in my confessions. My antiques are medals of foraging. I am eager to share with my guests the stories and, at times, the fables of my fabulous finds.

I once discovered, at a flea market, for less than $10, what is known as a cake train: a plasterware children's delight from the 1950s consisting of a train of circus animals, designed to be placed on top of a birthday cake. I cleaned it carefully and bought a cake (surely you didn't think I would bake one!) just to fit the wonderful cake train, with its lions and tigers and elephants. Yet when I presented it at dinner, the very people to whom I thought I was offering a special treat shuddered gently and declined. The cake train was — you know — second-hand. It was a reminder that one must not assume that everybody shares your taste or, in my case, a weakness for the wacky.

I have a great pumpkin bowl with dip tray ($3 at a thrift store), a beautiful 1950s silverplated coffee pot with cream and sugar on a tray ($5 at a church rummage sale), lovely little sterling silver coffee spoons ($2 each at a flea market), and whimsical napkin rings (the cloisonné set for $10 from Trader Jack at the flea market, the ceramic kitties for $6 at a discount kitchen store, the wooden bunnies found at 25¢ for a set of four at a garage sale). You can mix and match single floral plates for 25¢ to $1 each at garage sales. At a consignment store, I found a Fitz and Floyd bunny rabbit cheese server. The plate was blue and a pink rabbit sat at the side, with little serving knives for his ears. The delight of seeing my grown-up guests play with this bunny and laugh at the joy of that little fellow was worth one hundred times what I paid for him. I have extraordinarily beautiful platters, all found for a song at garage sales, sold to me by elderly women who no longer cared to use them and who were glad to pass them on to the next generation. Beautiful things, recycled, become more beautiful as they are enjoyed by another wave of consumers, cooks, and connoisseurs.

Linens can be dirt cheap at garage sales. (Of course, you will want to wash and iron them all over again once you get them home.) I often swoon at the sight of a set of dinner napkins, carefully folded and pressed, immaculate, pristine, perfect, set on a table at a garage sale and priced at 50¢ for the set. How can I leave them there? They want to come home with me and grace my next dinner party!

My dining table is a showpiece, bought second-hand by my parents in the 1940s. Alas, the chairs disappeared over the years. I make do with some execrable 1970s phony baloney rickety cookie cutter chairs from a department store. I am still waiting for the right chairs to show up at auction. Luckily, I have two Bentwood-style chairs to upgrade the joint, and only because I happened to be in a restaurant at just the right time. The restaurant was renovating and literally gave to the diners the chairs they were sitting on. I wish I could find more restaurants like that. (Fairmont Hotels, do you hear me?)

Part of the fun of decorating with antique and vintage finds is knowing that the objects will resonate with your guests in a way that the most modern, expensive furniture and china never could. Despite our sophistication, many of us are sentimental souls. Reminders of our childhood are powerful, and comforting. The great 1950s plasterware fruit cornucopia that my mother kept in the basement for 20 years has been hauled out and displayed in splendor on my kitchen wall, flanked by dozens of gloriously bright plasterware apples, grapes, bananas, cherries, and pears that I have found at ga-rage sales and flea markets. Any baby boomer entering my kitchen pauses, entranced, open-mouthed. I once found a guest in tears in my kitchen. He was standing in front of my spooner, a jar-shaped glass dating to the Depression era that holds teaspoons. His eyes glistened as he smiled. "I haven't seen one of these in years. It takes me back to my parents' kitchen."

The engraved wineglasses that were exiled to the same basement in the 1960s, because they were just too 1940s, now congregate in my kitchen cupboard and reign supreme at every dinner party. Guests hold them reverently and murmur, "What great wineglasses! Where on earth did you find them?"

"Style has nothing to do with money. Anybody can do it with money. The true art is to do it on a shoestring."

TOM HOGAN, AS QUOTED IN *SIMPLE ABUNDANCE: A DAY-BOOK OF COMFORT AND JOY*, BY SARAH BAN BREATHNACH

In the living room, my sofa is elderly but from a noble lineage and, not surprisingly, bears the marks of several generations of tiny fifth cousins leaping up and down on the upholstery. As far as I am concerned, the holes are badges of courage for the sofa. They are also proof that I do indeed have relatives, however energetic.

I also, unabashedly, have perfectly horrible things in my house, mostly from the times I have been at auction and did the whiplash shoot-yourself-in-the-foot routine when the auctioneer said, "First person to raise their hand —" and my hand went up before I realized the rest of the sentence was "buys this ugly, potholed, marked-up utilitarian telephone table that you will have to hire a van to take home and that you will end up moving from room to room in your home because you can't afford to hire somebody to cart it away."

Cheap cheap cheap. Make it your mantra if you are afraid of going bankrupt with a dinner party. Expensive is fine, when can you afford it. But if you can afford the time to go to flea markets, garage sales, and auctions, you may know the added benefit of finding something quirky and original for your home, something that might be hard to find in the average store and (this is the best part) for which you paid peanuts. Just take the advice Dennis Lakusta doles out in his hilarious song "Value Village Shuffle" and "remove the tag, remove the tag."

So even if you don't have a mansion or a trendy downtown loft, you can do well with something that is priceless: your very own style. Yes, you have it. It took me years to find my style. Even now, it is constantly in transition. Yet I surround myself with things that please me and am amazed when I look around my home and see what I have acquired on an artist's income. That pleasure — and amazement — is passed on to my guests.

Music: The Invisible Guest

Music is one of the great soothers or catalysts. What we hear sets our mood, sends us into tremors of tension, or settles us into serenity. Music holds our hand through difficult times, raises our spirits when we are blue, or transports us beyond our sometimes-trying reality.

I have attended maybe 225 parties too many in which the host's idea of a good time was playing non-melodic thumping rap or rock music at high volume. And maybe this is a good

> *"Let's sing! Let's eat!*
> *Let's jiggle our feet!"*
>
> Mary Engelbreit

idea, if you have an IQ in the two-digit range, if you are attempting transactions of an illegal nature and want to make sure people are so comatose they won't notice, or if you are performing pornographic acts on the dance floor. Not that I am criticizing these states or activities. I just have different ideas of what welcoming music is.

I am an old-fashioned sort of gal. I figure that if I have invited people to dinner, I want them to be relaxed, and sort of vibrating happily. And quietly. If my guests rarely rave about my cinnamon chicken, they do (with an enthusiasm that no doubt compensates for what they sometimes cannot cough up about my cooking) acknowledge my taste in music.

One learns (through eye-popping, and sometimes nauseating, experience) what not to play at dinner. For

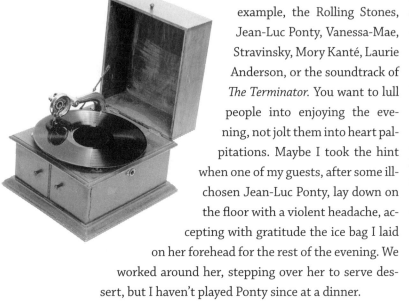

example, the Rolling Stones, Jean-Luc Ponty, Vanessa-Mae, Stravinsky, Mory Kanté, Laurie Anderson, or the soundtrack of *The Terminator*. You want to lull people into enjoying the evening, not jolt them into heart palpitations. Maybe I took the hint when one of my guests, after some ill-chosen Jean-Luc Ponty, lay down on the floor with a violent headache, accepting with gratitude the ice bag I laid on her forehead for the rest of the evening. We worked around her, stepping over her to serve dessert, but I haven't played Ponty since at a dinner.

The exception to this is the occasion when the meal is so dreadful that your last resort is playing something so irresistible that the hapless guests absolutely must get up and dance. I recommend the "Bongo Bong" cut from Manu Chao's *Clandestino* album, which is not only wonderfully danceable, but also so politically incorrect that your guests will be either galvanized into action or stunned into a horrified stupor.

Plan the music for the evening every bit as carefully as you create the guest list. I have stacks of CDs set out for each phase of the evening, in order. (See page 128 for some recommendations.)

The guests arrive in a flurry of activity, sitting tentatively, sizing one another up, sipping wine and munching appetizers, the expectation of the evening ahead like a blank canvas. Will it be dull? Amusing? Stressful? Rowdy? How will the evening evolve? What adventure awaits? How will the personalities blend and mix?

My favourite for appetizers is *Strictly for the Birds,* with Stephane Grappelli (my idol) and Yehudi Menuhin playing swinging violins on "Lullaby of Birdland" and "Bye Bye Blackbird." I can rely on these two masters for an inviting, charming, civilized atmosphere that says to the guests, "Relax, smile, have fun — be warm, easy, upbeat — all will be well — there is no heavy metal here." Excerpts from the *Quintet of the Hot Club of Paris* perk up the group, too, and sometimes a little bit of peppy Paul Whiteman and his orchestra sets just the right cheery rhythm. Try Antonio Carlos Jobim and his gentle bossa nova for a warm, welcoming rhythm and Madeleine Peyroux for a mellow mood with her soulful, swinging jazz ballads. There was a phase in my entertaining career when I played Claude Bolling pre-dinner. The conversation was always terrific: open, easy, free-ranging. I now realize that people leapt easily from one idea to the next because of the nature of the music, which was so flowing and joyful.

The important thing at this stage is to use music of cheerful charm: nothing threatening, noisy, or intrusive. This doesn't mean it has to be blah elevator music — simply melodic music that puts people at ease without offending them by being too mundane or weird. I love obscure African, Hungarian, and Brazilian music but have taken the hint when my guests' eyes glaze after a few moments.

Finally, after the cheese and crackers and jolly jazz, we move to the table: candles lit, napkin rings and silver gleaming in welcome, and of course, a zillion doodads on hand to distract the guests. For these opening moments, I recommend *The Best of Ofra Harnoy* (which contains some swinging cello renditions of Beatles standards) or the *Orford String Quartet Encores* to gently ease people into their chairs.

Consider the placement of the speakers. I have made the mistake of seating a guest who hated music right in front of a speaker. He complained vigorously and turned down the sound, which was a mighty inconvenience for the little cook, who was relying on the music as an ally in the battle for dinner. Yet others love music and delight in being right in front of the speaker that is emitting Fats Waller or Billie Holiday. You have to figure this out before, but if you know your guests at all, eventually you will get it right.

Set the music so it can be heard, but not so that it drowns out conversation. It should be an accompaniment to the meal, not a tyrant or a bully or a guest who insists on taking centre stage. I once had the misfortune of living across the alley from what appeared to be an infestation of bikers. (And mine is a nice neighbourhood. With trees. And a library.) While I attempted serene dinner parties, with thoughtful conversation, and Oscar Peterson in the background, booming bass and rap music throbbed across my yard, punctuated by screamed obscenities related to personal acts and family members. This was not only a clash of lifestyles, but also a definite bucket of ice water on my elegant evening.

Around the time that the food is passed and conversation begins (or continues) in earnest, I aim for music at once stimulating yet relaxing. If the food is a little off-key here or there, a mix of Oscar Peterson, Billie Holiday, and George Shearing ensures all is forgiven. Not too many lyrics, please, unless conversation dies a horrible death and you need a distraction. A nice compromise is the great Verve album *Louis Armstrong Meets Oscar Peterson*, with Louis and Oscar so laid back and perfect. Throw in some of the Nylons' quieter stuff from their first album and a few of the best tracks from Willie Nelson's *Stardust*. The idea is to keep people awake but not distract from the conversation with any drum solos or shouted lyrics or — perish the thought — acid jazz. If

> *"Life is a banquet, and most poor suckers are starving to death."*
>
> Mame Dennis in *Auntie Mame*, by Patrick Dennis

you want to listen to Glenn Gould playing the *Goldberg Variations*, do it in solitude, as it should be done, to savour every note.

Dinner is the crucial time for music. Too laid back, and the guests will doze off in their soup. (Anything by George Winston will send people into a coma — but keep it in abeyance as it is great for neutralizing brawls.) Too frenetic, and a certain nervous energy will ricochet around the table, with people sniping at one another or, worse, challenging one another to duels.

A sad commentary on modern manners is the fact that once I had a guest who manhandled my stereo. He stopped the music I had chosen (and it was my party and I chose it well) and rummaged through my albums until he found a rather loud country and western album (which I don't even remember buying) and put it on the turntable. I was surprised by how this upset me. It made a big (negative and annoying) difference, and I realized that not only did I view music as an

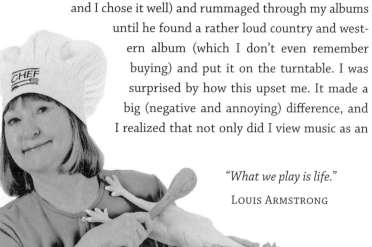

"What we play is life."
LOUIS ARMSTRONG

important part of the atmosphere of a party, almost like an invisible guest, but I also needed it desperately for myself, as my companion for the evening.

Once the main course and salad have passed without disaster, turn to coffee and dessert. By now, everybody should be feeling mellow and safe. Choose music that does not dwell on death, fire and brimstone, or like things. Do not, under any circumstances, pull out your treasured copy of *Carmina Burana*. All those monks sound sexy and intriguing, but I promise you, people will flee like rats from the ship if you inflict it on them. Nobody likes to be reminded of mortality, sin, and vengeance at dinner, even though my cooking may inspire such thoughts in the diners.

I like *Jazz Samba* with Stan Getz and Charlie Byrd, the quiet Brazilian rhythms of Antonio Carlos Jobim or Joao Gilberto. Chet Baker, Shirley Horne, and Ben Webster. P. J. Perry's *My Ideal* is fine, sophisticated late-night music. Try Bill Evans and Toots Thielemans' *Affinity* for piano and harmonica in easy melancholy; Sade for non-intrusive, gentle sadness; Steve Miller's album *Born 2B Blue* for quiet vocals, the Bill Charlap Trio, or some quietly swinging harp. Try the Jazz Moods series from Concord, which is no-fail uplifting yet tranquil jazz. You can't go wrong with Erroll Garner or Keith Jarrett. You, however, can go waaaay wrong by playing anything too experimental. I love the vocal stylings of Leon Thomas, jazz yodeller and spiritual healer, but I have noticed the way some people's eyes widen and freeze on the few occasions I have played it at dinner.

By this time, people are either ready to go home or — if it's a great party, an unqualified success (!) — they are having such a great time talking about life and death and art and culture and angst and society that they want to hang around. If, at 3 a.m., they are still sitting with their elbows on the table, talking and smiling, with the warmth of the candles lighting their faces, you can finally relax. This is a successful party. Paul Winter's *Wintersong* emanates warmth and forgiveness. Archie Shepp and Horace Parlan send quivers through the soul (for by now, the guests should be open, content, radiant with pleasure). *Duets for the Spanish Guitar* with Laurindo Almeida and Salli Terri is definitive late-night music, with gentle guitar and open, soaring soprano. Don't forget that great Verve series *Jazz 'Round Midnight*. (And, if you want to send a gentle hint, consider the great version of "One for My Baby," by Frank Sinatra with Nelson Riddle, which is like a musical nightcap.)

"Music washes away from the soul the dust of everyday life."

RED AUERBACH

Choose the music that expresses who you are, the

music that comforts you, because then you, as host or hostess, will emanate joy to the guests who arrive. My music is bossa nova or the rhythms of Cape Verde (Cesaria Evora or Teofile Chantre), which always put me in just the right mode of relaxation and happiness. (As a stranger in St. John's once said to me, "Bossa nova and a glass of wine — you can't go wrong.") Perhaps it won't speak to everybody, but as long as it isn't intrusive, it is likely that the good vibes of the little cook will infect the other guests, as well.

> "It don't mean a thing if it ain't got that swing"
>
> DUKE ELLINGTON
> AND IRVING MILES

The power of music is that whether or not people are consciously aware of it, they will be affected by what they hear. The music will seep into their ears, their pores, and if they are sensitive at all, it will be expressed in their conversation. It is a beneficial and therapeutic form of brainwashing. No murders will be committed at your dinner table when you play Charlie Haden.

My choices are personal. You know your friends and your taste: choose music that will make you happy and your guests feel welcome. Music will soothe the soul and defuse the bomb of a deadly dinner. People forgive much if you have chosen well. They may not know exactly why, but they will know they are relaxed and content, happy to be at your table.

the music menu

Cocktails: Lilting Welcome, Promise of Good Times

- Tony Bennett and k.d. lang, *A Wonderful World*, Columbia Records
- Bet.e and Stef, *Day by Day*, Bet.e and Stef Records
- *Café de Paris, Accordion Classics from the Boulevards of Paris*, Music Collection International
- Antonio Carlos Jobim, *Antonio Carlos Jobim's Finest Hour*, Verve
- The King Cole Trio, *The Best of the War Years*, Stardust Records
- Yehudi Menuhin, Stephane Grappelli, *Strictly for the Birds*, Angel Records

- Itzhak Perlman and Oscar Peterson, *Side by Side*, Telarc
- Madeleine Peyroux, *Careless Love*, Rounder
- Karl Roth, *Everybody Wants to Be a Cat*, THM
- Soweto String Quartet, *Zebra Crossing*, BMG

Dinner: Music to Dine By

- Toots Thielemans, *Chez Toots*, Private Music
- Various artists, *Destination Brazil, Sultry Rhythms of Corvocado Nights*, National Geographic, Sugo Music
- Various artists, *Dinner by Candlelight*, Jazz Moods, Concord

- Various artists, *Sounds of Winter, Jazz Moods*, Concord
- Various artists, *Bossa Nova Lounge*, IPANEMA, Dubas musica, Universal
- Various artists, *Nightcap Jazz*, Pacific Entertainment
- Carol Welsman, *Hold Me*, Avenue Jazz
- Jessica Williams, *The Next Step*, Hep Jazz

After Dinner:
Mellow Inside, Chilling Out
- Laurindo Almeida, *Duets with the Spanish Guitar*, Angel
- Louis Armstrong and Oscar Peterson, *Louis Armstrong Meets Oscar Peterson*, Verve
- Jeri Brown with special guest Leon Thomas, *Zauis*, Justin Time (only for those like their jazz with a little yodel)
- Bill Charlap Trio, *Written in the Stars*, Blue Note Records
- Bill Evans, *We Will Meet Again*, Warner Bros.
- Bill Evans and Toots Thielemans, *Affinity*, Warner Bros.
- Charlie Haden, *Nocturne*, Verve
- Keith Jarrett, *The Melody at Night, With You*, ECM
- The Nylons, *The Nylons*, Attic Records
- Frank Sinatra and Antonio Carlos Jobim, *Francis Albert Sinatra and Antonio Carlos Jobim*, Reprise
- Ben Webster, *Bounce Blues*, Past Perfect

into the fray

> "A good meal should be like a performance; the Edwardians understood that. Their meals were a splendid form of theatre, like a play by Pinero with skilful preparation, expectation, denouement, and satisfactory ending. The well-made play; the well-made meal. Drama one can eat."
>
> ROBERTSON DAVIES, *THE REBEL ANGELS*

The doorbell rings. The evening has begun. Strap your apron to your loins, down a glass, and open that door. The curtain is up! And the Rebel Cook must be ready for the performance. You are going to make your guests feel as welcome and valued as possible. Greet them warmly. Ignore the exploding sounds from the kitchen. (Alternate strategy: commandeer them into action as if only they could save the kitchen from self-immolating.) You are the leader of this adventure, and no matter how frantic and desperate you are, you must find a way to include your guests.

Always remember that guests are often just as nervous as you are. Sometimes, in my case, it is because they have been to my home before, and they remember the trip to emergency after the curried shrimp. But often it is because they are shy, apprehensive, wondering what they will say to whatever strangers they meet.

This is showtime.

It is at this moment that all your preparation is justified. The fretting, the recipes, the music, the appetizers, the décor — everything that you have anguished over serves a purpose (if you are somebody like me, but maybe you are a sort of throw-everything-around person, in which case why are you reading this book?). The guest enters and, after being greeted warmly by the host, is offered a glass of wine, invited to sit or stand, as they choose, and comforted by soothing music and an interesting environment.

> *"It is etiquette for a hostess to have a terrible stomach ache at three minutes past six and to* KNOW *that no one is coming."*
>
> VIRGINIA GRAHAM, SAY PLEASE (1949)

Showtime goes in stages: the greetings, the appetizers, the demented attempts to hide what is really happening in the kitchen, the dinner itself, then dessert and coffee, and then the denouement, when (if it is a successful party and people are not fleeing to their vehicles, scattering crumbs and uneaten pieces of carrot wrapped in napkins in their wake) people sit and chat

> "Of what happened later in the evening nothing definite here can be stated. None of the guests later on had a clear remembrance of it. They only knew that the room had been filled with a heavenly light, as if a number of small halos had blended into one glorious radiance."
>
> ISAK DINESEN, *BABETTE'S FEAST*

easily. There is a defining moment, known to every host and hostess, when one looks around the room and sees the joy in people's faces and knows all is well.

THE EARLY GUEST

A guest, under no circumstances, should arrive early. Early guests are a sin against the host or hostess. Early guests do not realize the havoc they wreak, along with the hyperventilation, the silent cursing, the panic attacks, and the desperate search for the beta blockers and the Prozac. Early guests are the people who either never entertain (lucky, feckless souls) or who are so organized in their own entertaining that it seems trivial to them to arrive half an hour early as it would not inconvenience *them* at all if you did it to them. These are not people you want as guests, as they would deviously lift cushions and furniture when you are out of the room, searching for dust, lint, and secret diary pages, such is their innate sense of superiority.

As for the former, people who do not entertain are lucky to be invited anywhere and therefore should be suitably grateful for whatever you fling on the table. The downside is that they retain, resolutely, a total lack of awareness of the rigours of entertaining and therefore have not the faintest sense of appreciation of what the little hostess endures in order to have them to dinner.

I once gave a dinner to honour two dear friends. Inept as I was, and despite the usual amnesia about the shopping list while at Safeway, I determinedly pushed my way to AT (Arrival Time, which is usually much earlier than DT, which is Dinner Time).

"A well-bred person always receives visitors ... but if you are occupied and cannot afford to be interrupted you should instruct the servant beforehand to say you are 'not at home.'"

THE HABITS OF GOOD SOCIETY (1859)

I had cleaned the house and was almost organized. Multitasking, swinging efficiently (perhaps an overstatement) from one chore to the other. Yes! The little hostess had everything under control! Until about an hour and a half before the guests were due, just after I had washed my hair and decided to open the wine. Didn't I deserve a drink as a reward for all my hard work? My corkscrew snapped in half. No problem. I had backup. Then corkscrew #2 (an inferior model but still serviceable) also snapped in half. Ever resilient, I ran downstairs in my Mickey Mouse sleepshirt and Halloween socks, towel over my wet hair, and found corkscrew #3 (always keep a corkscrew in your luggage), ran back up the stairs, and tried again. Corkscrew #3 glued itself inside the cork but did nothing else.

> *"When visits are attempted as 'agreeable surprises,' they are seldom very agreeable to the surprised."*
>
> COMPLETE ETIQUETTE FOR LADIES (1900)

At that moment, the doorbell rang. Two of the guests had arrived One Hour and a Half Early.

I sat them down with books and music, made a garbled call to another guest, ordering a corkscrew, and quickly dressed, flinging on makeup in a millisecond (only at the end of the evening did I discover that I looked like a clone of Clarabelle the Clown) and, heart pounding, began throwing dishes and silverware on the table, hoping it would all end up in the right places. So much for the beautifully set table in which I take such misguided pride. I had lost half an hour of valuable time with ministering to the early birds, to say nothing of the mortification factor.

At least the chicken is nearly done, I thought. Then I looked at the stove. Ten minutes before AT — although the oven was blazing away, the chicken, which I had been about to put in the oven some time ago (JUST BEFORE THE UNEXPECTED EARLY ARRIVAL OF THE FIRST GUESTS), was still sitting on top of the stove. I stifled my hysterics, threw it into the oven, turned up the heat, and prayed.

The other guests arrived and everything seemed to go well for a while: wine, cheese, olives, great music, lively conversation. I made sure the wine flowed freely enough that nobody noticed that the chicken was a little late making its entrance (DUE TO THE UNEXPECTED EARLY ARRIVAL OF THE FIRST GUESTS). When it did, it was amazingly delicious. And just in time, as one of the guests, an actor, chose my dinner table as the appropriate setting to accost another guest, a former theatre critic, on a review of 15 years ago. The pall that began to settle over the chicken was counteracted by the words of praise for the beautifully set table. Ha.

As I put on coffee and tried to coordinate the serving of three separate birthday cakes, two of the guests, quite tipsy (thanks to my earlier efforts to delay the meal, BECAUSE OF THE UNEX-PECTED EARLY ARRIVAL OF THE FIRST GUESTS), started to wash the dishes, trying to be helpful. I was three rooms away when I heard the THUNK! What made the THUNK! was the largest roaster, overturned, on the kitchen floor, with chicken garlic juice covering a quarter of the kitchen floor and two square feet of the (once-pink) hallway carpet. The two dish washers were frozen, simply star-

ing at the overturned roaster as if they were watching a horror movie with mildly detached disinterest. They would have been sober had it not been for THE UNEXPECTED EARLY ARRIVAL OF THE FIRST GUESTS.

I grabbed every paper towel and dishcloth in the kitchen and began desperately wiping up the mess. Perhaps this is what distracted me from the coffeemaker. When I finally cleaned up the floor and went to serve coffee, I discovered that the coffeemaker (which had been perfectly fine for the last four years) was spewing coffee grounds and coffee all over the counter, so that all china, tins, and ornaments were sitting in a pool of freshly brewed coffee. I braved electrocution, unplugged it, and somehow served the coffee.

While the guests enjoyed their coffee and birthday cake in the dining room, the little cook uncorked another bottle of wine and proceeded to drink like a fish in the kitchen.

I barely remember the rest of the party. (I think I sang, which certainly speeded the departure of the hapless guests.) I do remember being incredibly relieved when the last guest left. I wondered what I could have done to avoid this disaster.

This is it: Invest in high-quality locks, deadbolts with an alarm system. If your doorbell rings before the appointed hour, do not, under any circumstances, open the door, even if it is a group of fire fighters with hoses and axes and sirens in the background. Trust me, they are just inconsiderate dinner guests trying to get in early. Some people will do anything to ruin the evening.

As I am inept and always late with dinner, I prefer that guests arrive a considerate 10 to 15 minutes late. Is that too much to ask? And I also prefer that they sit and talk among themselves in the living room while I fall apart in the kitchen. The latest I have ever served dinner is 9:30. I don't feel so bad about this when I remember that one of my friends began the road to divorce when she eventually served dinner to a group of 10 very hungry people at midnight. Her husband was furious, but she was like me, a Rebel Cook, one who tried vainly to entertain. In her case, she lost the battle, or the race.

THE ABSENT GUEST

At the opposite end of the spectrum is the guest who *never* shows up.

We all know the horror of a last-minute cancellation. I have found myself screaming like Billie Burke in *Dinner at Eight*, "What do you mean, you aren't coming!" One plans the dinner, sets the table, and

> *"A dinner invitation, once accepted, is a sacred obligation. If you die before the dinner takes place, your executor must attend the dinner."*
>
> WARD MCALLISTER, *SOCIETY AS I HAVE FOUND IT* (1890)

then somebody calls half an hour before dinner and says they are unavailable? I once had a guest cancel at five minutes past the appointed hour for a luncheon that I had spent four hours of the prime years of my life preparing. It reminded me of an article in *Vogue* many years ago, written by Joan Juliet Buck, in which she said clearly that good manners is about keeping appointments, fulfilling obligations, and returning calls.

A socialite in Philadelphia once sat her dog at the table when a guest cancelled so that the number at table was not 13. I would personally go for a stuffed animal, but I understand the concept, which is not new. In 19th-century Paris, an institution called the Quatorziemes consisted of men who dressed to the nines every evening and waited at home, ready to dash off to any dinner where the number of guests sank to 13.

An invitation is a contract between the host and guest. We all violate this contract at times (even I, to my embarrassment, have done so). However, ultimately, the secret to maintaining a place in the social circuit of your friends and acquaintances is to consistently fulfil this agreement.

In this, there must be appreciation and respect for

the efforts made by each other. And, in this case, that means that the absent guest should have some awareness of the ways in which the hosts have expended themselves in order to create a civilized event. The host must also appreciate that the guest has set aside this time from their busy life to attend the party.

Although many of us have had moments in which we have been so out of sorts that the thought of socializing is a horror, we may consider these thoughts: perhaps if we went out into the world and interacted, there might be a chance of making a social or spiritual connection that would lift our spirits and remind us we are not alone in our despair — or perhaps we would feel better knowing we have the strength to behave well, no matter what.

Under no circumstances am I advocating that we are obliged to attend events that are unpleasant or displeasing to us, if not necessary. But I am saying that if one is obliged to cancel, it is only polite and considerate to do it well before the appointed hour. Or at least have a reasonable excuse. Death, illness, and a lottery win being the most acceptable.

DANCING AT THE DOOR (THE SOFT SHOE SHUFFLE)

So there they are, at your door, bearing wine, we hope. They are probably feeling a combination of eagerness, relief, shyness, anxiety — all those mingled emotions

the ideal guest

The ideal dinner guest arrives bearing a bottle of wine. Several bottles are very nice and never a mistake. I have noted that the more frequently people dine at my place — and return — the number of bottles increases with each visit, perhaps in proportion to their fear of what might be awaiting them on the table — or perhaps by their realization that dinner may be A Long Time Coming.

The ideal dinner guest does *not* arrive bearing flowers, unless they are already prettily arranged in a vase. Anybody who has ever entertained knows well the feeling of your little heart sinking while the corners of your little mouth turn determinedly upward at the sight of a beautiful but beastly inconvenient bouquet of flowers in their wrapping — which means the pots will overflow, the kitchen will smoke, the veggies will explode, and, worse, the guests' glasses will go empty and their coats unhung while you forage for a vase and arrange the flowers, oohing and aahing diligently all the while.

on entering a strange abode and wondering what awaits them. (Of course, if they have been to dinner at my place before, their faces may also reflect the apprehension of the unknown horror ahead of them.)

You, as host or hostess, greet them warmly. You step back from the door, not blocking their way into the house, and offer to take their coats. As a single person hosting a dinner, I invariably end up holding eight coats on my less-than-muscled arms, nearly passing out while trying to introduce people, convey bottles of wine to the kitchen, and make vague little gestures of welcoming hospitality.

You are indeed blessed if your hallway closet is located at the entrance, so you can dimple becomingly at the guests as you hang up their coats. My hallway closet is a good 20 paces from the front door. I spend the first hour of a dinner party trotting back and forth, laden with coats. Another solution is to designate a guest, one of your dear friends (and, we would hope, such a desirable creature would always be among your guests), as a helper. Ask this dear friend to take up the slack, to collect coats, pour drinks, and do the things that you, as nervous host, are already hyperventilating

"Etiquette is an art — the art of doing and saying the correct thing at the correct time — the art of being able to hold oneself always in hand, no matter how exacting the circumstance."

LILLIAN EICHLER,
BOOK OF ETIQUETTE (1921)

about. If you don't have a dear friend in the mix, grab somebody by the collar and tell them they are going to do this for you. This is amazingly effective. (I note that, surprisingly, sometimes the most reserved of guests blossom under this responsibility. It gives them something to do. It relieves their shyness. And it helps the little hostess.)

Another note: count the hangers before the party. (No, I am not hinting that anybody is going to abscond with them.) Sometimes family members appropriate hangers without informing the rest of the inhabitants of the home. I have had too many experiences wandering through the hallways like Heathcliff on the moors, calling out for hangers while trailing guests' scarves, coats, and gloves.

Next, we come to the tricky problem of footwear. And it is a messy challenge for those of us who live in wet or frosty climates.

The world is divided into two sorts of people: those who have servants and those who do not have servants. These people are immediately identifiable when they enter their home. People who have servants do not do any cleaning and assume that the fairies come in the middle of the night and clean their carpets and their hardwood floors. Also, if they can afford servants, they can also afford new carpets every year or so. They never remove their shoes — laden with dust, dirt, mud, snow, cow manure — when they enter a home, because they assume the little host has servants as well.

The rest of us, the poor peasant Rebel Cooks, must slave like serfs with various odious and smelly cleaning products to keep our floors in respectable condition. Consequently, when we enter a home, we automatically slip off our shoes because we are sensitive, compassionate people who immediately imagine the hardship invoked on the host or hostess by our muddy feet. Another aspect of this is the consideration of foul and pestilent diseases lurking out there that, although not always attached to footwear, could conceivably come dancing into your home on the soles of a feckless guest who has just tromped through unspeakable offal or radioactive material. Not that I am paranoid or anything. I just read a lot of magazine articles that inform me on the dangers of modern life.

Therefore, there is the golden moment at the door. The window of opportunity. It seems to me that any person of any sense at all would look at a gleaming hardwood floor and recently vacuumed Oriental carpets and swiftly slip off their shoes. Alas, this is not the case. I have swooned with horror as arriving guests (without a swipe or wipe of their clodhoppers) have willfully tracked mud across my just-cleaned living room and dining room.

I know somebody, a man of exquisite taste and many fine heirloom rugs, who claims that not once, *not once*, has a guest come into his home and failed to remove shoes. "It has never been an issue," he told me. "They look around and immediately see what they should do." Now, I ask you. What is wrong with me that I have a few friends who do not grasp this? I love them anyway, mind you, but maybe just a little less when I am on my hands and knees cleaning the floor after they have tracked 168 autumn leaves, 16 footprints of mud, and something that looks like cat doodoo across my floors.

So, you have several choices: you can look delicately at their feet as you take their coats, and they, wanting to please you, will slip off their shoes. Or you can be more blatant, as in "Would you care to wipe your shoes? I just cleaned the floor." Or, even more desperately, "Oh keep your shoes on. I don't mind getting down on my hands and knees cleaning the floors at three in the morning after you leave."

Next problem. Cold Feet. Do we really want our little guests to suffer with blue and purple tootsies, just to save our floors? No, we do not. The answer is a large, aesthetically appealing basket of slippers by the door: slippers in every size, bought cheaply at your local discount store. Let your guests choose, and if you are feeling really generous, give the slippers as a gift for them to take home. If they are nice slippers, it is great incentive for guests to remove their shoes.

Such a dilemma — so many of us go to parties gussied up, not wanting to ruin the effect with cheap dollar-store slippers. This is a battle between fashion and compassion for the hostess. I haven't solved it, and I urge somebody more brilliant than I am to write a book that does. I am extremely fond of guests who whip off their caked boots and produce a fetching pair of soft-soled shoes, Immaculate and Pristine. I recently purchased a lovely pair of hostess slippers, and I now heartily concur with the view that those of us who are foolish enough to live in subarctic climes might consider having a set of shoes Just for Hosting and Guesting.

Another tip: if your guests are courteous enough to discard their footwear on arrival (and to re-apply same footwear on departure), ensure the lighting at your entrance is sufficient to ensure that they can identify their shoes.

One of the most inconvenient episodes in my shabby career as a hostess was the time an elderly woman wore the wrong pair of shoes home, and then resolutely refused to admit it. The pair of shoes she left behind were two sizes too large for my elegant friend Bianca, yet Bianca had to slop along in them as we drove to the home of the two-sizes-larger-but-not-admitting-it guest. After much discussion, argument, and debate, it was finally agreed that the shoes that fit Bianca were indeed hers (Ralph Lauren loafers), while the generic flats belonged to the elderly (and stubborn) myopic. This is what is known as the Travelling Hostess, when one stands in front of car headlights in crisp autumn air, two miles from home, breath curling above one, comparing shoe sizes to ensure that all ends well, and the shoe fits.

THE CHUMMINESS BEGINS

Once people enter a room, they generally want to sit down, get comfortable, engage in chitchat. You perform introductions in the most practical way possible. If you were raised with traditional manners, you present the gentleman to the lady: "Mary, this is Peter Pepper." Or you introduce each person to the group as the person arrives, which is practical in that you repeat all names several zillion times, which makes it easier for people who don't know one another to remember all those monikers. One book recommends dialling your home number from your cell and leaving the names of the people who you should remember, which seems to me to be just about one of the most outlandish pieces of advice I have ever heard, but, wait a moment, if my memory gets any worse ... hmmm.

Some people like to shake hands, which, in my opinion, is an increasingly unsanitary practice. Where have those hands been? And do their owners have a cold or West Nile Virus? Have they just petted a dog or cat? And now they are going to touch the cheese knife? And how are you going to wash yours without making a big deal out of it? When I have a moment, I am going to join one of those anti–hand shaking groups and make the world a safer, better place. And a more aesthetically pleasing place. (I am not alone in this. I have recently read about 29 magazine articles about why handshaking should be abolished, especially considering the expected advent of various predicted plagues and pandemics.)

I am all for hugging if you know people well. Hugging is much safer than hand shaking and makes people feel good all over. A hug goes a long way toward mellowing people in the dinner department. One should note though that some people just hate being hugged, and you have to respect that. You can usually tell those people. These are the ones who, when you hug them, feel somewhat like a stop sign that has been planted at the side of a deserted road for about 10 years and is totally immovable.

> *"The hand that holds the highball is a damp and clammy mitt."*
>
> PEG BRACKEN, *I TRY TO BEHAVE MYSELF: PEG BRACKEN'S ETIQUETTE BOOK*

Good Spirits

Good spirits make good spirits. One way to ensure this is to offer your guests a beverage or three shortly after they arrive.

Designate an assistant in this task. Often this will prevent a shy person from climbing behind the sofa or playing with the fringe of your carpet. It gives them something to do and an excuse to talk to everybody. People like to feel useful, and pouring wine while the little host or hostess frets in the kitchen is supremely useful. I am especially fond of those guests who assume this responsibility without being asked.

I was once invited to a soirée where I knew only the host and not a soul of the other 10 people. For some reason, the host kept forgetting to bring me a glass of wine, although he constantly replenished the drinks of others. (I refuse to believe it had anything to do with my colourful past at his parties.) Finally, I was a desperate woman and had to purr, in as sweet a tone as I could manage from my parched throat, "Wine, please?"

Do not reduce your guests or yourself to this sad state. I sometimes make a blanket statement to the assembly that as a desperate Rebel Cook, I am on call in the kitchen and therefore unable to be the perfect prescient hostess, and I implore them from the bottom of my little harried heart to help themselves to wine, water, or whatever if I become absent-minded.

They're lucky I remember to get anything on the table, let alone appear with a bottle the moment a glass is empty.

I am not advocating that one force alcoholic beverages on those who do not drink for reasons of health, taste, or religion. No matter how desperately you are choking the cauliflower in the kitchen, try to retain some sensitivity to your guests.

Having said that, there is much more to be said of the wisdom of oiling the rest of the guests, the ones who do drink, with a nice wine before dinner. If you are serving anything above plonk, it is advisable to fill the wineglasses only half full. And don't refill until they are empty, for a number of reasons, including the very obvious one that if you serving several wines, you might well pour a very fine pinot noir into an indifferent chardonnay.

If this were a serious book on entertaining, this chapter would contain several nice recipes for exotic cocktails. And a real cook would probably skip into the

"What is the first thing a bachelor host must remember?

Never be in the kitchen mixing drinks as your guests arrive. Greet each and every one. After all are there, mingle with them. In order to do this, if no servant is on hand, designate a bachelor friend (more than one if needed) to pitch in and act as bartender, empty ash trays, and clear away used glasses and generally make himself useful."

CAROLYN HAGNER SHAW,
MODERN MANNERS: ETIQUETTE FOR ALL OCCASIONS (1958)

> "A host at a table where a guest is obliged to ask, is a host dishonored."
>
> BARON LÉON BRISSE, *LA PETITE CUISINE DU BARON BRISSE* (1870)

kitchen and whip up cute cocktails with 27 ingredients, two sessions with the blender, and pop little pink umbrellas into each one, by which time the guests will have turned to stone in the living room waiting for their drinks.

I will give you one (1) cocktail recipe, from *Hering's Dictionary of Classical and Modern Cookery,* the classic tome on wine and cookery:

"Absinthe cocktail: 3 parts absinthe, 2 parts water, 1 teaspoonful sugar syrup, a dash of anisette, 4 dashes Angostura, a twist of lemon over each cocktail."

I selected absinthe because it seems sort of exotic and dangerous and makes me want to wander down the Champs-Elysées on the arm of a sexy accordion player with a moustache and a beret. Unfortunately, if you served this, there is a good chance you might poison your guests and/or get arrested, so I include it only for its obscure charm.

However, you don't need to serve absinthe to get a reputation. I once attended a dinner where the after-dinner treat was Armagnac. I was madly impressed and assumed that the host always had Armagnac on tap. At another home, I was offered calvados, which is incredibly potent and elegant, and once more assumed this was the lifestyle of the host. Then I served what one guest characterized as "a lethal Hungarian liqueur" at one of my parties, and suddenly I had A Reputation. Yes, I was a daring woman with risky tastes in liquor. This reputation was enhanced by the fact that this Hungarian pear liqueur could probably lift an elephant's ears if you breathed on it after drinking it. I blew out the candles, just in case.

How I admire people who can pull of the fancier stuff. I once visited friends who served delightful cocktails non-stop, each one lovingly crafted in a blender and served in vintage cocktail glasses, with dear little paper napkins adorned with hula dancers. They had a jukebox playing golden oldies in the background. Frankly, I have no recollection of what they served for dinner, not because of overindulgence, but because I was so enchanted with their presentation. When you entertain, find something you love and do it.

I love reading long lists of wine pairings with gourmet dishes, lists that call for a fine Bordeaux or a haughty sauterne. I suddenly imagine myself serving a 15-course meal and pouring fine wines into crystal glasses while my guests ooh and aah over my sophistication. Yes! Then reality

> *"Serve this dish with much too much wine for your guests, along with some cooked green vegetables and a huge salad. You will be famous in about half an hour."*
>
> JEFF SMITH, THE FRUGAL GOURMET

strikes with a cruel backhand, and I sink into my chair and contemplate the implications of that list. First of all, I would have to sell my car to supply all that wine. And second, there is the terrible thought that I might have to cook dishes to meet the standards of the wine.

This is when I haul out the newspaper and check to see what decent wine is on sale at the discount liquor store. A terrible confession: I buy what is drinkable, cheap, and on sale, and pray fervently that guests bring wine. Then my choices are simple. "White or red?" or "Chardonnay or shiraz?"

I also like to serve wines made by famous winemakers who I have actually met. It makes me feel like a celebrity. And that I am throwing a celebrity party. And, in a way, I am. Because if I like people enough to invite them to dinner, they are celebrities in my life. Another advantage of meeting the winemaker is that people get the impression you have a glamorous lifestyle and know something about fine wines if you can say, casually, "Oh yes, the winemaker was very pleased with the grapes last year." Name-dropping is shallow and meaningless in the Big Picture, but we are talking about the small picture here, the Rebel Cook at table, trying to fool her guests into a good time.

And if you want an entertaining, basic guide to wine drinking, watch the film *Sideways*, which, aside from its considerable merits as a study in character and wit, is an ode to wine. At one point, one character coaches another in the rituals of sniffing, twirling, and inhaling a wine. The day after watching it, I suddenly started inhaling and twirling the perfectly ordinary wine hanging around in my refrigerator.

THE GLORIOUS GRAPE

Whatever you do, just make sure you don't serve a truly inferior wine. Years ago, at an achingly dreadful party at some sort of suburban nightmare of a home, where the company was so boring that I fervently needed a good glass of wine, I nearly gagged when I tasted the hosts' pride and joy, a nice crabapple wine made in their very own backyard. This, I should emphasize, was before the days of the glorious winemaking stores that taught people how to make a decent wine.

"In the Victorian era, however, a rigid social order made compiling guest lists a painstaking task. Planning a social event involved complex stratagems, since the proper mix of people at a party was an important means of demonstrating social aspirations. Social climbing was a full-time occupation for those who had made new fortunes in industry and who were anxious to be accepted in to Society."

MARILYN HANSEN,
*ENTERTAINING IN
THE VICTORIAN STYLE:
REFRESHMENTS,
SETTINGS, EVENTS*

The first sip glued the insides of my cheeks to my tongue and I abandoned all dignity, following the hostess around the room as she brandished a bottle of Hochtaler in one hand and the odious homemade wine from hell in the other. I jockeyed around her, trying to reach the Hochtaler. This was how low I had sunk. Instead she grandly poured me another glass of the backyard wine.

I should note that perhaps I am prejudiced against homemade wine because my mother, despite being a nondrinker, when she was pregnant with the little Rebel Cook, obligingly drank some homemade fig wine when out to dinner, which sent us both to the hospital with toxemia, and we both nearly died. This is the sort of thing that can turn a person off figs and homemade wine, even though everybody tells me that it is only a prenatal memory and I am silly to insist it made me what I am today. Ha. Now, in the new age of excellent homemade wines, I have had guests bring wonderful bottles of their own vintage to parties, and the good name of homemade wines has been restored.

A bestselling author I know is one of the best guests

ever. Not only because he has cachet, and pretty good table conversation, but because when he isn't writing book after book, which people grab from bookshelves pronto (I should be so lucky), he is in his basement making wine. Really good wine. And he comes to dinner bearing four or five bottles of it. One must ensure that one knows guests like this. This is the sort of guest who is always guaranteed a place at my table.

Another one of my evergreen guests is a single gentleman, somewhat shy, extremely energetic, who consults his favourite wine shop before coming to dinner and who invariably brings a topnotch, faint-as-you-sip, float-into-reverie bottle of wine. His wine choices have made many a fine dinner, and he, too, is on my list of no-fail guests.

Despite my hints that guests be encouraged to bring wine (and there is absolutely nothing wrong with jumping up and down a few times when you see the bottle, and maybe planting a large loving smack on their nearest cheek), don't pout if they don't. One whiff of my cooking and they usually show up with three bottles next time in self-defence. Hope springs eternal in the Rebel Cook.

To Each Their Own

Perhaps you are hesitant to entertain because you don't have a set of matching wineglasses. I guess there must be people in this world who do, and good for them. But if your guests are any sort of fun at all, they are not going to be putting their energy into mentally matching up the glasses and deciding your stock is inadequate.

I have eight engraved wineglasses from the 1940s, which were my mother's and are quite beautiful. I also like the diversion of an assortment of wineglasses, some single florals from Spain, Hungary, or Italy, some utilitarian peach glass from France, some Czechoslovakian crystal, and some very plain crystal wineglasses found at the neighbourhood thrift store for 50¢ each.

"A sophisticated diner looks upon a colored wine-glass with horror."

MARGERY WILSON, *THE POCKET BOOK OF ETIQUETTE* (1937)

A big advantage of using eclectic, mismatched glasses is that it is so much easier to keep track of who is drinking what when you are dazed in the kitchen (and perhaps with a glass or two already in your system), frantically trying to serve wine and keep an eye on whatever is about to explode on the stove.

The Power of the Word

We must now consider the art of conversation, which requires certain skill at improvisation. Scripted lines

history to the rescue

Even if there is not a first-class wine on the table, you have a fallback position. Any bottle of wine is enhanced when you haul out your silverplated wine coaster and place it casually on the table. It may not seem like much, but it elevates whatever you are drinking.

You can find wine coasters cheaply at specialty stores or even flea markets, or you can go the distance and spring for an antique sterling silver Victorian wine coaster, which I did years ago and have never regretted it. Every time I see that glorious openwork coaster of elegant and aged sterling on my table and realize that families dined around it more than 100 years ago, I experience a wave of sentiment and satisfaction. And if I share that thought with my guests, they look at the coaster with new appreciation.

can be used as a framework but can turn a promising party dull as the dishwater sure to be used later. I am constantly confounded by what supposedly civilized people think passes for conversation. How bright do you have to be not to insult a person's clothing, hairdo, religion, or profession on introduction? Or am I just living in a Jane Austen sort of fantasy world? There are various age-old conventions to consider. They may

> *"The table is a meeting place, a gathering ground, the source of sustenance and nourishment, festivity, safety, and satisfaction."*
>
> LAURIE COLWIN, AS QUOTED IN *SIMPLE ABUNDANCE: A DAYBOOK OF COMFORT AND JOY*, BY SARAH BAN BREATHNACH

seem stodgy, but they make perfect sense, even today.

Do not talk politics, religion, or money at dinner. Under the influence of nervousness or alcohol, I have done at least one of those and have seen my name removed from guest lists. And I deserved it.

Having learned these hard lessons, from etiquette books and personal experience, I recognize their wisdom. A friend once said to me, as I planned a dinner, "Oh just get people talking politics, and things will go well." She never entertains, so she did not recognize the folly of this. Talking politics or religion leads you down the road to a deadly evening, where either people never speak to one another again or, even worse, fall asleep from terminal boredom. I have observed that people who like to talk politics or religion generally do so from an overwhelming desire to hear the sound of their own voice pontificating on important matters, seldom from a real desire to communicate or learn about the rest of humanity.

Well, then, let's play games! Excuse me? In my humble opinion, those people who like to play games at dinner parties should just rent a video and not bother with other people. I personally am not interested in carrying on in the kitchen for four hours (after eight hours of cleaning) just to play Trivial Pursuit. Parlour games are for people who either know one another so well that they (insultingly) feel they have nothing more to learn or for people so limited socially that they are afraid of real conversation.

One of my performer friends once complained to me, "I am never going to another dinner party where I have to play charades. The host thinks it will be a great thrill. Well, excuse me, this is what I do for a living, interpreting and creating and performing. I do not want to do this on a social occasion."

Most of us have the naive notion that talking to somebody about their profession will be of interest to them. Humbling as it may be, we should accept the reality that anything that we, the uninformed but marginally interested, have to say about a business (such as brain surgery or floral design) that the other guest has invested maybe 10 years of education and another 10 years of experience in is not going to be revelatory or even vaguely interesting to them. Unless you have such

"One must not take advantage of the fact that everyone is pinned to his or her chair for the duration of the meal; one must not, for example, ask pointed questions, or questions requiring long replies."

MARGARET VISSER,
THE RITUALS OF DINNER:
THE ORIGINS, EVOLUTION,
ECCENTRICITIES, AND MEANING
OF TABLE MANNERS

a colossal ego (and so many of us do) that you think your uninformed utterances will be hypnotically fascinating. Perhaps you will also be gifted with the sight of somebody committing hari-kari before your eyes, rather than endure one more second of conversation with you. Does this tell you something?

The exception to this is when you are genuinely interested in another person and their life and the questions you ask are respectful and inquiring. They can usually tell, intuitively, your intention and respond accordingly. Most of us have endured so many meaningless conversations at parties that when the Real Deal comes along, a conversation in which the other person is interested and actually connects with you, it is cause for celebration. One goes home and tallies the conversations. "Yes, I had two good exchanges." Maybe I am a lone little voice in this, but I assess my outings based on how I connect with other souls. And if nothing happened, it was either me (perhaps a bad mood) or an environment that wasn't right for me. (For example, biker bars or a hockey game.)

Most of us are reticent on occasion. Before this shyness renders your guests motionless or sends them into the hall closet to hide among the coats, find ways to tell them that they've been invited because you value them. You also might delicately remind them that, as guest, they have a role to play. Assign them a person to charm and entertain. ("Oh, Josh has just broken up with his wife. She left him for twins. And women, at that. His medication doesn't seem to be working. Could you chat him up a bit? Just don't let him near the cheese knife.")

I will never forget the look on my friend Barbara's face when she met my taciturn friend Phil. They were the first to arrive, and as I puttered anxiously in the kitchen, I heard Barbara in the living room, bravely trying to pull words out of Phil, much the way one digs turnips out of the garden in the fall, when the ground has almost frozen. This was her task, and I suffered with her as I ministered to the chicken over the stove, listening to each foray into conversation she attempted. The pleasant, eager questions. The monosyllabic responses. The leaden silences.

> *"Conversation should be as varied and as charming as a beautiful bouquet to which everyone who comes has brought a flower."*
>
> LUCIE HEATON ARMSTRONG, *ETIQUETTE-UP-TO-DATE* (C. 1924)

Suddenly she appeared beside me, her usually serene eyes the size of demented dessert plates. "Wine!" she hissed. She grabbed the bottle, sloshed about a pint into her glass, and disappeared back onto the battlefield of conversation with Phil. (Unbelievably, they later became lovers and didn't do much talking, but did an awful lot of drinking and shouting, and then broke up and never spoke to each other again. Full circle. And I started it all.)

A really safe way to enter into conversation (other than the weather) is to ask a person about themselves in a way that is not intrusive. For example, do not say "What do you think of the new herpes tests?" This is not a good idea. But you could ask a generic question that could open the door to different kinds of responses, spiritual or anecdotal, such as "What do you enjoy most about parties?" or "What is the best party you have ever attended?"

"To invariably commence a conversation by remarks of the weather shows a poverty of ideas that is truly pitiable."

S. A. FROST, *LAWS AND BY-LAWS OF AMERICAN SOCIETY* (1869)

Most people love to talk about themselves. But there are some people who do not. One has to learn to identify the two groups and respond accordingly. This sounds like a lot of work, and it is, but socializing successfully is work. That is why some people are brilliant at it and always get asked to parties and others are Crossed Off the List. (Trust me, the person who insulted my best friend at my last dinner party has gone down to #85 on my guest list.)

Dinner conversation can be crushed to pieces by bores. Into the category of Bores, we can stuff the bigots, the bullish, the shallow, the silly, the pompous, the argumentative (or, even worse, the combative), to say nothing of those who arrive bearing weapons and insults. The perfect hostess must have the talent of finding a way to stretch out the hook without embarrassing or hurting the guest. Some older etiquette books suggest urging said guest to play the piano. My suggestion is looking upward, rising from the chair in intense horror, and whispering, sotto voce, "Is that a bat flapping around the chandelier?"

To repeatedly invite a brittle or sarcastic person to dinner (as I once did) is to ensure that the evenings will end early and invitations will be undertaken with reluctance. Many years ago, I didn't realize why my dinner parties had suddenly become so lethal (and it wasn't the cooking, I swear) until I realized that one person was the unwitting cause, because all conversation was met with her loud disdain and laughter. She thought she was being charming and cosmopolitan. I thought she was being the Guest Who Is Disagreeable. And I was waaaaay too slow to drag out the large felt

"The Success of a Dinner: A host and hostess generally judge of the success of a dinner by the manner in which conversation has been sustained. If it flagged often it is considered proof that the guests have not been congenial; but if a steady stream of talk has been kept up, it shows that they have been smoothly amalgamated, as a whole. No one should monopolize conversation, unless he wishes to win for himself the appellation of a bore, and be avoided as such."

ETIQUETTE, RULES AND USAGES OF THE BEST SOCIETY (1886)

> *"The true art of being agreeable is to appear well pleased with all the company, and rather to seem well entertained with them than to bring entertainment to them."*
>
> *ENQUIRE WITHIN UPON EVERYTHING: A VICTORIAN ALMANAC* (1856)

pen and cross her name off my list. Because I was the Cowardly Hostess and felt I was obliged to ask her because she was a lonely sort of woman. It was around then, in my rapidly descending career as hostess, that I decided to balance compassion and self-preservation.

Bottom line: invite the right people, the interesting and interested, and conversation will take care of itself. The best of guests realize that the host or hostess has invested considerable effort, time, and money in creating a special evening. The guest who ruins it through boorishness or bore-ishness is deservedly banished. The philosophy is simple but potent.

SEND THEM HOME SAFELY

After all this talking and munching and eating and drinking and oiling and showering with liquor, you may want to consider the wisdom of sending your guests out onto the road with all this booze in them. You want to entertain, not decimate, the local population.

One should aim to have the sort of party that invokes warm and delightful and hilarious memories, not the sort of party that has various guests sitting bolt

bad manners at table

Bad Manners
    at Table
Tips back his chair.
Eats with his mouth too full.
Feeds a dog at the table.
Holds his knife improperly.
Engages in violent argument
    at mealtime.
Lounges upon the table.
Brings a cross child to the table.
Drinks from the saucer, and laps with this
    tongue the last drop from the plate.
Comes to the table in his shirtsleeves, and puts
    his feet beside his chair.
Picks his teeth with his fingers.
Scratches her head and is frequently unnecessarily
    getting up from the table.

FROM A 19TH-CENTURY ILLUSTRATION, IN *THE NIGHT 2000 MEN CAME TO DINNER AND OTHER APPETIZING ANECDOTES*, EDITED BY DOUGLAS G. MELDRUM

upright in bed at regular intervals for the next 10 years, remembering the horrific and humiliating moments they created under the influence of the grape.

If your guests do not have designated drivers (and I note that more and more people are teetotallers today, so in fact you may have a large sober contingent, worse luck for you in the dinner department), then bring on the coffee, tea, herbal tea, and water.

"One more drink and I'd have been under the host."

DOROTHY PARKER

Although no etiquette book I have read recommends it, this is my book and I am recommending it: Have a large pitcher of ice water and glasses on the table so that people can pace their drinking and ease their livers with some healthy refreshment. It is particularly useful at the end of the evening. Some people don't want coffee (although I always offer decaffeinated coffee, as well as regular, and am surprised when people are extraordinarily grateful that I would think of such an obvious choice for those of us who don't want to be vibrating in our beds with post-party jitters until dawn), and some are allergic to all those little plants in herbal tea. Pour, and pour, and pour whatever guests desire until you can ascertain that all are sober before departure.

The most important point regarding liquor is that if you are a Rebel Cook, you must have a drink awaiting you at the end of the evening. Whether it was a failure or a success, only you know how you have suffered and anguished and wept and thrown yourself on the floor in despair to create it.

Then, when the door closes behind the last guest, the host, like an actor who has just seen the curtain come down on a great performance, uncorks the bottle in her dressing room and drinks a toast.

"Hospitality warms the cockles of the heart, draws us nearer to that level on which all humanity may meet. To talk together in a spirit of congenial festivity, to eat and drink with our fellows, keeps us normal in a world careening around political curves at a dizzy pace. To share what we have clears the cobwebs of selfishness and self-consciousness from the mind engaged in its own pursuits and sweetens and freshens all life."

MARGERY WILSON,
*THE POCKET BOOK OF
ETIQUETTE* (1937)

desperate measures
and simple solutions

*T*ake your favourite pen and write onto these pages the names of your favourite takeout places and caterers:

Caterers & Takeout

· ·

Name: _____

Telephone: _____

Delivery Time: _____

Name: _____

Telephone: _____

Delivery Time: _____

Caterers & Takeout

. . . .

Name: _____

Telephone: _____

Delivery Time: _____

Name: _____

Telephone: _____

Delivery Time: _____

Name: _____

Telephone: _____

Delivery Time: _____

Name: _____

Telephone: _____

Delivery Time: _____

Name: _____

Telephone: _____

Delivery Time: _____

acknowledgments

*T*hanks to all the friends and relatives who have sat around my table and gamely eaten all the stuff I have served, no matter how mysterious it was. Thanks to all the guests who behaved strangely at my table and in my home. I had no idea how handy those anecdotes would become, years later.

Thanks to Jennifer Pringle and Paula Oreskovich for wine tips. Thanks to Kathy Richardier and Gail Norton for giving me an entrée into the world of food writing (even though they both know I know nothing about it but they still printed my words in *City Palate,* a wonderful magazine about food and cooking). And further thanks to Kathy and Gail for giving permission to use their recipes and thoughts, just as I thank Sharon

Cook of the Swivel Collective for permission to quote from *Plots & Pans*. More thanks to the friends who sent me notes on just why they were brave enough to come back to dinner again and again chez Kupecek. A special thanks to Elizabeth Duffey, for here support and encouragement.

A huge thanks to Stephen Hutchings for laughing at what I write. He has the gift of encouraging the creative spirit. And thanks to Kara Turner for laughing, too. People who laugh at our jokes are the very best sort of friends and associates. And special thanks to Lori Burwash, a wonderful and gifted editor who not only knows how to craft words in a sensitive way, but seems to think I am sort of funny.

Finally, a big thank you to my mother, who loves to laugh, and loves to cook. She never taught me a thing about cooking, but she sure taught me a lot about laughing.

PHOTO CREDITS

The photographs of me in my demented glory were taken by the talented Bill Vauthrin. I thank him for that, and for the rubber chicken. All other photos are courtesy of Photos.com.

books that inspire, inform, or intimidate

*T*hese are some of my very favourite books, which have helped me out of many a kitchen jam. Mostly I just like to recline and read them, but every now and again, a frantic prowl through the pages has saved my bacon, my chicken, or my soul.

Bickel, Walter (ed.). *Hering's Dictionary of Classical and Modern Cookery*. Giessen, Germany: Fachbuchverlag Dr. Pfanneberg & Co., 1958.

Bracken, Peg. *I Try to Behave Myself: Peg Bracken's Etiquette Book*. New York: Harcourt Brace and World, Inc., 1963.

Bracken, Peg. *The I Hate to Cook Book*. New York: Harcourt Brace and World, Inc., 1960.

Bradshaw, George. *Suppers and Midnight Snacks*. New York: David McKay Company, Inc., 1969.

Breathnach, Sarah Ban. *Simple Abundance: A Daybook of Comfort and Joy*. New York: Warner Books Inc., 1995.

Colwin, Laurie. *More Home Cooking: A Writer Returns to the Kitchen*. New York: HarperCollins, 1993.

Coudert, Jo. *The I Never Cooked Before Cookbook*. New York: Signet, The New American Library, Inc., 1963.

Driver, Elizabeth (intro.). *The Home Cook Book: Canada's First Community Cookbook* (125th Anniversary Edition). North Vancouver: Whitecap Books, 2002.

Eichler, Lillian. *Book of Etiquette*. Garden City, NY: Nelson Doubleday, Inc., 1921.

Fisher, M. F. K. *The Art of Eating*. New York: Collier Books, 1990.

Graham, Virginia. *Say Please*. London: The Harvill Press, 1949.

Hansen, Marilyn. *Entertaining in the Victorian Style: Refreshments, Settings, Events.* New York: Penguin Group, 1990.

Hawthorne, Rosemary. *Do's & Don'ts: An Anthology of Forgotten Manners.* London: Pavilion Books, 1997.

Hill, Amelia Leavitt. *The Complete Book of Table Setting with Service, Etiquette, and Flower Arrangement.* New York: The Greystone Press, 1949.

Holmes, Marie. *Glamour and the Hostess: A Guide to Canadian Table Setting.* Toronto: Northumbria Sterling, n.d.

Meldrum, Douglas G. *The Night 2000 Men Came to Dinner and Other Appetizing Anecdotes.* New York: Charles Scribner's Sons, 1994.

Rowinski, Kate (ed.). *The Quotable Cook.* New York: The Lyons Press, 2000.

Shaw, Carolyn Hagner. *Modern Manners: Etiquette for All Occasions.* N.p.: E.P. Dutton & Company, 1958.

The Swivel Collective. *Plots & Pans: The Book Club Cookbook.* Toronto: Sumach Press, 2002.

Visser, Margaret. *The Rituals of Dinner: The Origins, Evolution, Eccentricities, and Meaning of Table Manners.* Toronto: HarperCollins Canada, 1991.

Watson, Lillian Eichler. *The Standard Book of Etiquette.* Oyster Bay, NY: Garden City Publishing Co. Inc., 1948.

Wilson, Margery. *The Pocket Book of Etiquette.* N.p.: Frederick A. Stokes Company, 1937.

about the author

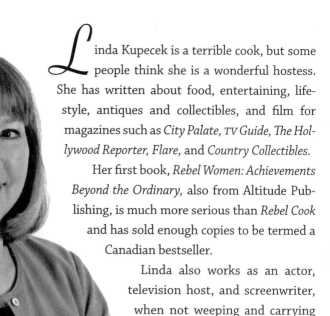

*L*inda Kupecek is a terrible cook, but some people think she is a wonderful hostess. She has written about food, entertaining, lifestyle, antiques and collectibles, and film for magazines such as *City Palate, TV Guide, The Hollywood Reporter, Flare,* and *Country Collectibles.*

Her first book, *Rebel Women: Achievements Beyond the Ordinary,* also from Altitude Publishing, is much more serious than *Rebel Cook* and has sold enough copies to be termed a Canadian bestseller.

Linda also works as an actor, television host, and screenwriter, when not weeping and carrying on in the kitchen.